S0-BAY-379

The Beautiful Wives Cookbook

GLITTERING RECIPES FROM CELEBRITIES' KITCHENS

By Mrs. Earl Wilson and Ruth Pool

PRENTICE-HALL, INC.

ENGLEWOOD CLIFFS
NEW JERSEY

designed by
Linda Huber Purnell

◄§ THE BEAUTIFUL WIVES COOKBOOK §►
Glittering Recipes from Celebrities' Kitchens
by Mrs. Earl Wilson and Ruth Pool

© 1970 by Rosemary Wilson and Ruth Pool

Copyright under International and Pan American
Copyright Conventions

All rights reserved.
No part of this book may be reproduced in
any form or by any means, except for the inclusion of brief
quotations in a review, without permission in writing
from the publisher.

ISBN 0-13-072900-0

Library of Congress Catalog Card Number: 72-119513

Printed in the United States of America *T*

Prentice-Hall International, Inc., London
Prentice-Hall of Australia, Pty. Ltd., Sydney
Prentice-Hall of Canada, Ltd., Toronto
Prentice-Hall of India Private Ltd., New Delhi
Prentice-Hall of Japan, Inc., Tokyo

*There is
no spectacle on
Earth more appealing than
that of a beautiful woman in the act
of cooking dinner for someone she loves.*

Thomas Wolfe, THE WEB AND THE ROCK, 1939

Kissing don't last; cookery do.

George Meredith, THE ORDEAL OF
RICHARD FEVEREL, 1859

Introduction
by

EARL WILSON

A HUSBAND IS expected to make
humorous or caustic remarks about his wife's
bumbling attempts at cooking, but I cannot, for Mrs.
Earl Wilson is one of the truly inspired amateur chefs of the Jet
Age and the Supersonic Society. I should know because I have en-
countered hundreds of amateur chefs in my travels. The trouble
was, so many of these amateur chefs thought they were professional
chefs, and they still do.

That's why I look forward to dinner at home, where I am usually
served at the kitchen table about two feet from the gas grate and
the oven. There is nothing fancy about *la cuisine Rosemary*.

"Be here by eight," my chef commands, and if it's eight-o-five,
I don't have time for a cocktail because the Beautiful Wife miracu-
lously operates on some timetable arrangement by which eight
means eight. Hurling my jacket into a corner—the kitchen always
seems to be at oven temperature, a point I would like to bring up
at a later day—because it's not too comfortable in the 100° New
York summers, I slide down and grab a paper napkin, to shouts
of, "Come on, get started, eat it while it's hot!"

"You want a drink?" I timidly inquire.

"*No!*" Mrs. Wilson is far from a prohibitionist, but in cooking she wants to be in complete control of herself at all times.

"I think I might have one," I say, pouring one.

"Eat it while it's hot," she scowls. She's a female octopus as her eight arms deposit on the table hot rolls, cole slaw, mashed potatoes, baked beans, gravy, turnips, rutabaga, and maybe cranberry sauce and baked apple with marshmallow on top, completely encircling me.

"How'm I gonna eat my way out of here?" I ask. "I've only got one stomach."

I shudder as I say this, thinking she could honestly answer, "Yes? Well from here it looks like two."

Is the cooking art hereditary? I only know that my Gorgeous Mother-in-Law, Rosella Lyons, was one of the great cooks in the world and that her daughter has, thanks to modern methods and modern application, improved on some of her creations.

They had their own foibles. Rosella used to chase her daughter out of the kitchen while cooking. Wanted no kibitzers.

Now my wife chases *me* out of the kitchen.

Once I tried to photograph the B.W. cooking Thanksgiving dinner. We always refer to that meal as Turkey à la Busted Flash-bulb.

Thinking back to the days when she was just a gay young girl (and I was a gay caballero), I would say that the most surprised person about her becoming a great cook is me.

I urged her to write a cookbook. A cook should pass on her secrets and not just cook for herself and her husband. How sad it would have been if Leonard Bernstein had never conducted except in the shower!

Foreword
by

ROSEMARY WILSON

THIS BOOK CONCERNS me
and my eating and also my cooking. It all started
pretty modestly in 1936. Thirty-four years later, I realize
it has been my good luck to have eaten in all parts of the world
with many celebrated people. "I'm licking my chops," to use an
old family expression, over the masterpieces of the most talented
chefs of our time. Why not pass along some of the good things I
was privileged to learn?

But I must tell you the first of my cooking experiences.

My first meal in our own apartment after my marriage was
cooked by Earl—in a frying pan.

It was lunch. It was hamburger, beans, and fried potatoes, all
in one skillet, and that frying pan wasn't divisioned. It was pretty
good considering that it was the bridegroom's first meal.

Now came the bride's turn. I rushed home from my stenographer's job. I invited a friend for the dinner I was going to cook.
(She'd given us a toaster as a wedding present.) This time *I* was
cooking the meal.

The menu was simple: pork chops, mashed potatoes, creamed
corn, and gravy.

I threw off my office working clothes, peeled the potatoes, flopped them in the pot, put some salt in, then thought how bland potatoes can be, and added more salt, opened the can of corn, put it over the fire and now started frying the pork chops.

When the corn began to scorch, I became so occupied with it that I forgot to watch the pork chops when I mashed the potatoes.

When my attention was eventually drawn back to the pork chops, I tried to take them from the pan and found they were brittle, stiff, and dried. I had a terrible time trying to get them to stay on the plate. They wanted to slide off onto the floor, but I wouldn't permit that! How would it look—the bride's first dinner?

I busily made gravy. I cheerily called out, "Come and get it!"

They did.

The pork chops would not allow themselves to be cut because they were sliding all over their plates. The corn didn't taste bad if you didn't mind the scorch. The mashed potatoes were so salty they were almost pickled. I comforted myself, thinking, "The gravy will absorb most of the salt" until I remembered I had made the gravy with the potato water.

With tears in my eyes and not much money in our pockets, we went out to a cheap restaurant to have the bride's first dinner.

That's when I decided to learn to cook.

Foreword
by
RUTH POOL

MY DEAR FRIEND Rosemary and I
have enjoyed being "cooking buffs" for a
long time. We do not pretend to be professionals. We
enjoy good food, fun food—fun to eat, fun to cook, and fun to
serve.

Looking back on *the* book, one tends to forget some of our problems with menus and "testings" and to recall the many laughs we shared.

There was the month that four people sent in practically duplicate menus and each one thought "the other one" should be asked to change.

We discovered that some of the best cooks don't really know how much of anything they put into a recipe—or how long it takes to cook.

One discouraging week, we went through three solid days of failure—nothing but fallen soufflés, burnt desserts, raw meats. We were almost ready to give up. And then a delightful menu (I'm not going to mention which) came in. It was perfect. We were so surprised and happy that we called it a day, opened a bottle of champagne, and celebrated.

Arroz con Pollo Cugat
Vegetable Mélange Salad
Red Wine
Melon
Strong Coffee with Cognac

XAVIER CUGAT IS a true Spanish gourmet, but he particularly loves the cooking of his native Barcelona.

When he married Rosario Pilar Martinez Molina Baeza, popularly known as Charo, he was very worried that the dishes of her native city, Sevilla, would not be as good as those of Barcelona.

"I will teach you to cook Arroz con Pollo my way," he informed his bride.

Her Spanish temper rose, and she said, "But first I will cook for you the best Arroz con Pollo you have ever eaten."

Dubiously, Cugie let her go ahead and, much to his amazement, Sevilla could match Barcelona.

Arroz con Pollo Cugat

2 chickens (about two pounds each)
Olive oil
1 large onion (sliced)
1 green pepper (remove seeds and slice)
1 red pepper (remove seeds and slice)
2 cloves garlic
Pinch of saffron

1 cup chicken broth (canned or cubes)
1 cup white wine
⅓ cup water
1 cup uncooked minute rice
1 chorizo (this sausage may be bought in any Spanish store; if not available, a highly spiced sausage such as pepperoni will do as well)

Cut chickens in small pieces. Fry in olive oil until brown on all sides and cooked through. Remove from frying pan and put aside. Scrape drippings from bottom of pan and stir with the oil. If chicken has used all of the oil, add enough to fry the onion, peppers, and garlic until brown. Remove garlic from pan.

Heat saffron in chicken broth. Place all ingredients except chicken, rice, and chorizo in earthen casserole or heavy iron pot with cover. Slice sausage into casserole and add rice. Let simmer (covered) over a low fire until rice is thoroughly cooked. Add chicken and wine and simmer until chicken gets the taste of the rice (about ½ hour).

Cugie tells us that the above dish is served mainly during the week. But on weekends, especially on Sunday, all manner of shellfish is added—shrimps, mussels, clams, lobster. This is then called *Paella Valenciana*.

We experimented with still another version of Arroz con Pollo and found it quite delicious. We added to the recipe two eight-ounce cans of tomato paste and an extra bouillon cube. This we simmered along with the sausage, vegetables, and wine until slightly thickened (about 1 hour). We then added the chicken and simmered over a very low flame for another hour. Instead of adding the uncooked rice, we separately cooked packaged Spanish rice according to directions. We placed the chicken on the rice and poured the very rich gravy over it all.

❧ Vegetable Mélange Salad ❧

2 tomatoes   2 raw carrots (diced)
1 cucumber   Lettuce (chopped)

Combine all ingredients and marinate in wine vinegar, a little
olive oil, a pinch of sugar, and salt and pepper to taste.

❧ Melon ❧

Cugie says any fresh fruits will do for a dessert but melon is
preferred, especially Spanish melon.

❧ Strong Coffee with Cognac ❧

Add half a jigger of Spanish cognac to each cup of very strong
coffee.

Honduran Beans Heiser
Link Sausages
Pineapple and Pear Salad
Frozen Cheese Soufflé
Coffee

In 1936, the year *Gone with the Wind* made such a sensation, Dr. Victor Heiser, of tropical medicine fame, wrote *An American Doctor's Odyssey.* Dr. Heiser outsold Margaret Mitchell, and motion picture studios made numerous overtures to him. But he was much too busy and interested in what he was doing to ever pursue the offers that followed him to remote corners of the world.

It was while Dr. Heiser was traveling in Honduras that he came upon a small restaurant run by an elderly lady. She served only one dish, but people came from all over Central America to enjoy it.

She was taken ill one day and Dr. Heiser prescribed for her. In grateful appreciation, she gave him her only possession of value—her secret bean recipe—on the condition that he would not reveal it in Central America.*

When Dr. Heiser heard about this cookbook, he very kindly unearthed the bean recipe for us from his diary. It was dated

---

* *Editors' note:* This little old Spanish lady was doubtless unaware that a very similar dish to her beans is made in Mexico, using black beans.

January, 1927. Inasmuch as over forty years had passed, he felt there could be no objection to printing it.

We have added to the dish an extended menu that most certainly was not included in Honduras.

❧ *Honduran Beans Heiser* ❧

1 pound red beans
1 clove garlic

1 teaspoon salt
Hot sauce

In water to barely cover, simmer beans over slow fire for 4 or 5 hours or until beans become as soft and mushy as jelly. During cooking add salt and garlic. Keep checking water and adding more as it boils away, but only a little at a time.

When finished, remove beans from kettle and mash with a rolling pin until almost dry. Form into cakes and fry in deep lard until crisp. Serve with a hot sauce. (A hot barbecue sauce may be used, or you may make your own.)

Hot Sauce

1 cup mayonnaise
1 can tomato paste
2 tablespoons Worcestershire
    sauce
Dash Tabasco sauce
½ tsp. dry mustard

1 tsp. prepared mustard
½ tsp. chili powder
1 tablespoon vinegar
1 tablespoon brown sugar
Salt, pepper (to taste)

Combine all ingredients and let stand at least 1 hour to marinate.

❧ *Link Sausages* ❧

Simmer links in small amount of water in covered skillet for 5 minutes. Do not prick with fork. Drain off water and fry gently until brown and crisp on all sides.

❧ Pear and Pineapple Salad ❧

Fill pear halves with chunks of pineapple. Serve on lettuce leaves with French dressing. We recommend putting a dash of curry in French dressing whenever you're using it on fruit.

❧ Frozen Cheese Soufflé ❧

2 eggs
¾ cup very finely grated
   sharp cheese

½ pint whipping cream

Separate eggs. Beat yolks until creamy and lemon colored. Add cheese and then medium-whipped cream. Fold in stiffly beaten egg whites. Taste at this time to see if you wish to add a pinch of salt.

Place in refrigerator for at *least* 5 to 6 hours.

Steak au Poivre Mardnao
Fried Rice and Mushrooms
Hearts of Palm Salad
Fresh Pineapple with Rum
Coffee

Out in the hot soggy Philippine jungle one lunch time, movie actor Michael Caine was making do with the commissary buffet—but thinking in gourmet terms.

"Best pepper steak I ever ate was at the Mardnao grill at the Sheraton Hotel in Manila," Caine told my husband. He took us there for dinner that night, where I took notes on how this dish was prepared.

I hadn't known that Michael was so interested in cooking that even the size of the vessels was important to him. During the dinner he told us he had angered the Hong Kong girls by supposedly saying that while they had good legs, they were flat-chested.

Michael denied he had ever said it. Brushing it off, he said, and this is where his knowledge of dishes (of all sizes) comes in: "It was just a tempest in a C cup."

❧§§❧ Steak au Poivre Mardnao ❧§§❧

½ to 1 inch thick club steak
2 tablespoons butter
2 tablespoons parsley butter
2 tablespoons chopped onions
2 tablespoons chives
1 tablespoon fresh ground
   pepper

Pinch thyme, rosemary
1 jigger brandy (optional)
1 jigger red wine
2 tablespoons commercial
   brown gravy
2 tablespoons sour cream

Fry steak in plain butter. Remove steak from skillet and pour off steak and butter juice. Melt parsley butter and one by one add all ingredients with exception of brandy, wine, brown gravy, and sour cream. Stir very well after each addition, until sauce is smooth and ingredients are disintegrated. Stir in brandy and wine. Add brown gravy and stir. Add sour cream and blend all together. Replace steak just long enough to warm.

❧§§❧ Fried Rice and Mushrooms ❧§§❧

2 cups long-grain rice
Cooking oil

6 large mushrooms (chopped)
1 tablespoon butter

Cook rice in boiling salted water. Then fry in cooking oil until brown. Add chopped mushrooms that have been sautéed in butter. Combine. If you wish you may add more oil to the rice and cook the mushrooms while browning the rice.

❧§§❧ Hearts of Palm Salad ❧§§❧

1 can hearts of palm
2 tablespoons vinegar
3 tablespoons olive oil

Salt, pepper (to taste)
1 chopped hard-cooked egg

Slice hearts of palm in half lengthwise and lay on plate. Combine vinegar, olive oil, and salt and pepper and pour over hearts of palm. Sprinkle chopped hard-boiled egg over top.

❧❦❧ *Fresh Pineapple with Rum* ❧❦❧

1 fresh pineapple (use canned   1 jigger rum
* if fresh is not in season)*

Cut pineapple in desired sections. Pour rum over sections and serve ice cold.

Heavenly Chocolate
(Alias Gogul Mogul)
Angel Balls

We've all heard of great cooks, but how about one who always cooks with a 55-carat square-cut diamond on her delicate hand? It's the truth. Vala, wife of Ernest Byfield Jr., does.

Her father-in-law, Ernie Byfield Sr., along with his partner, Frank Bering, were the grand gourmets and wits of the Ambassador East and West hotels and Chicago's famous Pump Room. It is said of the room that everything is served flambé, "including the waiter's thumb."

Vala is of Russian descent and claims that Gogul Mogul was a favorite of the Czarina of Russia.

We've renamed it Heavenly Chocolate because that is what it is.

✿ Heavenly Chocolate ✿

2 *eggs (separated)*	1 *cup confectioners' sugar*
1/3 *teaspoon salt*	2 *or 3 drops vanilla*
1/3 *teaspoon cream of tartar*	*Cocoa (according to package directions)*

Have eggs at room temperature. Add salt and cream of tartar to egg whites and beat until mixture forms rounding peaks. Beat in ½ cup sugar, a tablespoon at a time, and continue beating until sugar is dissolved and mixture forms glossy pointed peaks (about ten minutes). Add the vanilla and continue beating 2 or 3 minutes. (You're right. This is a meringue recipe.)

Beat the yolks with remaining ½ cup sugar, a tablespoon at a time, until it's heavy and thick enough to float on top of the cocoa (also about ten minutes beating time). Place the yolk mixture on top of the cocoa and top with the egg white mixture. You will need to use a spoon first before you can drink this. On a cold wintry night you might wish to add some cognac to the cocoa.

❧ Angel Balls ❧

You may have come across this recipe under various names in other cookbooks. It has been in our files for over thirty years, so you can see it's not a new one. But because it's such a perfect accompaniment to the chocolate, we think you may want to try it.

1½ cups cake flour	¼ cup ground pecans
2 tablespoons powdered sugar	¼ teaspoon vanilla
¼ pound butter	

Mix all ingredients until you can roll the mixture into balls—or crescents if you wish variety. Bake for 20 minutes and roll in powdered sugar while hot.

If you would like to be a little bit different, you might try wrapping the dough around half a pecan instead of mixing it in, or even doing both.

Crème Senegalese
Scrambled Eggs Considine

It could be that part of the inspiration for great recipes is alcohol.

Bob Considine, one of the very great columnists, reporters, and authors, usually combines his breakfast with his lunch. Walking into "21" one noontime with his gay and amusing wife, Millie, he immediately ordered a double "Bloody Bull." That's vodka mixed with equal parts tomato juice and beef consommé. "Very nourishing," Bob comments. Millie joined him, but only with a single.

Finishing that and their soup, they ordered scrambled eggs. The cart was brought before them, and with a great flourish the maitre d' prepared the eggs at the table. Bob looked. "Got any chopped chives to stick in?" he asked. The chives were brought. "And how about some catsup on top?" Bob examined the dish. "Now, if you'd just toss some crisp, chopped bacon on top of that, it would be great."

People sitting around watching were fascinated. Many ordered the same. And so was born Scrambled Eggs Considine on the "21" menu for all to enjoy.

Crème Senegalese

3 ½ cups chicken stock
   (or cubes)
1 cup chopped chicken
½ teaspoon curry powder

4 egg yolks
2 cups cream
Salt, white pepper (to taste)

Bring chicken stock to a boil. Add chicken and curry powder. Beat egg yolks until creamy and lemon colored. Stir in 2 or 3 tablespoons of the hot stock and then the cream. When this is all thoroughly blended together, add it gradually to the rest of the stock. Stir constantly over a very low flame until soup is creamy and well mixed. Cool first and then chill. This is usually served cold. (Serves 4.)

It is only fair to tell you that when you add the mixture to the soup stock, it is possible for curdling to occur. If this should happen, pour the soup into a cold bowl placed in chopped ice and beat vigorously.

We highly recommend a most delicious facsimile of this. Dilute canned cream of chicken soup with cream. Add curry powder and chopped chicken.

⋘ *Scrambled Eggs Considine* ⋙

8 eggs
1 teaspoon salt
½ teaspoon pepper
8 tablespoons milk or light
  cream

2 tablespoons butter
2 tablespoons chopped chives
4 tablespoons catsup
2 tablespoons chopped crisp
  bacon

Mix eggs thoroughly with fork. Add salt, pepper, and milk or cream and mix again. Melt butter in skillet, tilting skillet so butter is well distributed. When hot, pour in mixture and reduce heat. Cook slowly, and gently lift cooked part of the egg so liquid can flow to bottom. Cook until all is set but egg is still moist. Avoid constant stirring. Remove to warm platter. Mix in chopped chives. Pour catsup on top and then sprinkle on the bacon.

Hors d'Oeuvres Voisin
Broiled Steak
French Peas
Custard

"Voisin? It is Paris away from Paris," say the international travelers and habitués of this restaurant at 30 East 65th Street, New York City.

We were lunching there one Sunday when much to my delight in came the late President Kennedy, along with Mrs. Kennedy and her sister, Princess Lee Radziwill. The President's Secret Service men had arrived a couple of hours ahead and had installed a phone line so he could be reached immediately from the White House. The Secret Servicers then went into the kitchen, watched the light switches, the cooks, the people coming in.

I was so excited, I told Earl, "Do everything just like the President. Eat everything just like he does."

The first part wasn't hard. A couple of Scotches. So far, fine! Hors d'oeuvres—minute steak medium rare—mashed potatoes....

"But I don't eat mashed potatoes," Earl protested.

"If it's good enough for the President——"

Then French peas. Caramel custard with lots of cream. Demitasse with lots of sugar.

The check came. "You want me to do everything just like the President?" Earl asked with a twinkle in his eye.

I watched horrified as he signed the check "John F. Kennedy."

Hors d'Oeuvres Voisin
(From the Tray Cart)

CAULIFLOWER SALAD: SAUCE
VINAIGRETTE AUX FINES HERBES

Cook a cauliflower head in small amount of boiling salted water. Remove green leaves and separate into flowerets. Drain and chill. When thoroughly chilled, sprinkle over cauliflower a mixture of oil, wine vinegar, salt, pepper, oregano, and dry mustard. Add mixture of chopped parsley, tarragon, chervil and chives.

SALADE DE CONCOMBRES

Pare cucumbers and slice very thin. Marinate with salt for half an hour. Drain thoroughly. Season with salt, pepper, oil, and vinegar.

SHRIMP WITH COCKTAIL SAUCE

Drop shrimp into salted boiling water to which fresh black pepper and an herb bouquet of dried basil, parsley, and thyme have been added (and garlic, if desired).

Cover tightly. Simmer about 7 minutes or until shrimp are pink. Drain and remove shells and devein.

Cocktail Sauce

One part mayonnaise to two parts chili sauce. Dash of Tabasco and Worcestershire sauce. Salt and pepper to taste.

CHEESE-COVERED SLICED TOMATOES

Cut tomatoes in generous slices. Sprinkle with oil, vinegar, salt, pepper, and Roquefort cheese.

❦ Minute Steak ❦

Voisin cooks its steaks in a charcoal broiler. Lacking that facility you may sauté yours in a combination of hot fat and butter in a skillet. With a steak about a half inch thick, 2 or 3 minutes on each side should do for medium rare.

Or, if you prefer, they may be broiled. Set your oven for broiling and preheat at least 10 minutes. Line the broiler pan under the rack with aluminum foil and turn up the edges to catch the drippings. When the steak is done to your liking, pour the juices over it and add salt and pepper to taste. A small pat of butter may be placed in the drippings along with a dash of Worcestershire sauce.

However, no matter what you do, a steak prepared at home is not going to look like one prepared in a fine restaurant. My housekeeper, Carrie, told me a little secret. Sprinkle black pepper and paprika over the steak and the color will improve. I tried this, and while I can't say it comes out looking charcoal broiled, it does look more appetizing. Be careful, though, to use only a little paprika or you'll end up with it being reddish brown.

❦ Mashed Potatoes ❦

Boil unpared potatoes (one to a person) until tender. (You may test with fork.) Drain, place over low heat, and shake for one or two minutes to dry out. Then peel and mash thoroughly, gradually adding warm milk and butter until they are fluffy and creamy. Salt and pepper to taste.

I personally find the instant mashed potatoes work just as well and are simpler to do.

❦ French Peas ❦

Place peas in boiling salted water to which a pinch of sugar has been added. Water should only be about half an inch over peas. Boil gently, uncovered, adding more water if needed (when peas are finished there should be barely any water left at all). Add butter. A little dried mint or parsley may be sprinkled on top.

❧ Caramel Custard ❧

1 pint milk

¼ cup granulated sugar

5 eggs, beaten

1 teaspoon vanilla

Bring milk to boil. Stir in sugar and beaten eggs. Take off fire. Add vanilla. Pour into custard cups. Place cups in pan of water (water should be nearly three-quarters up side of cups). Bake for about 20 minutes or until toothpick inserted in center comes out clean. Serve with cream. These proportions will serve 7 or 8.

Champeach Voisin
Eggs Benedict
Hearts of Palm with Voisin Dressing
Soufflé au Chocolat
Coffee

I'm sure you'd never forgive me if I omitted what the radiant and beautiful Jacqueline Kennedy had for lunch that day.

❧ *Champeach Voisin* ❧

1 split champagne Voisin
3 ½ halves of drained canned peaches
  (the smooth kind so there is no pulp)
2 heaping tablespoons shaved ice

Pour champagne, peaches, and shaved ice into an electric blender. Operate blender at slow speed for five seconds, then switch to high speed for fifteen seconds. This will serve four cocktails.

Hy Uchitel—the owner, no less—was kind enough to tell us an American champagne would do just as well and taste as good.

This drink can be made with ginger ale, and it is a delicious nonalcoholic drink.

❧❦ *Eggs Benedict* ❧❦

Eggs (one or two per person)
Dash of salt or vinegar
English muffins sliced in halves
Thin-sliced cooked ham (one
   slice per half muffin)

Hollandaise sauce
Thin slice of truffle or ripe
   olive

Be sure your eggs are fresh or they won't poach. Put a dash of salt or vinegar into just enough water to cover egg (this coagulates the egg faster). Be sure the water is very hot, and then either use an egg poacher or else give the water a twirl in the center of the pan and drop egg into the whirlpool. This will hold the egg together.

The Italians and French often poach their eggs in olive oil, which gives a good flavor and a creamy color. And so you don't miss out on anything—poaching eggs in consommé is also delicious.

Toast and butter half of an English muffin and place a thin slice of ham on top. The egg goes on top of the ham, and the whole concoction is covered with hollandaise sauce. Top with slice of truffle or ripe olive.

❧❦ *Hearts of Palm with Voisin Dressing* ❧❦

1 can hearts of palm
2 teaspoons salt
1 teaspoon fresh pepper
1 teaspoon paprika
¼ teaspoon powdered sugar
   (optional)

½ teaspoon powdered
   mustard
Dash cayenne
¾ cup olive oil
¼ cup vinegar

Slice hearts of palm in half lengthwise. Mix dry ingredients together. Slowly pour oil into dry ingredients, stirring all the time. Then stir in vinegar and continue stirring. Pour over hearts of palm. A slice or two of pimento may be placed across top for color.

❧❧ *Soufflé au Chocolat* ❧❧

2 ounces Maillard chocolate	¾ teaspoon salt
2 cups cold milk	4 eggs (separated)
½ cup sugar	2 tablespoons butter
⅓ cup sifted flour	2 teaspoons vanilla

Grease bottom of 2 quart casserole or soufflé dish.

In top of double boiler over simmering water, heat 2 ounces chocolate and 1½ cups milk until chocolate is melted and milk scalded. Blend and set aside.

Combine sugar, sifted flour, and salt. Gradually stir in remaining ½ cup cold milk. Add to mixture in double boiler. Cook over simmering water until thickened, stirring constantly. Continue cooking 5 to 7 minutes, stirring occasionally.

Meanwhile, beat 4 egg yolks until thick and lemon colored. Stir about 3 tablespoons chocolate mixture into beaten yolks. Put yolk mixture in double boiler and cook 3 to 5 minutes, stirring constantly. Remove from heat and blend in butter and vanilla and set aside.

Beat 4 egg whites until firm. Fold chocolate mixture into beaten egg whites and put in soufflé dish. Place dish in pan of boiling water and bake at 350° for 1 hour. Serve immediately, either plain or with sauce.

SOUFFLÉ CHOCOLAT SAUCE

1 pint vanilla ice cream (melted)
1 cup whipped cream

Combine and serve on the side.

Turtle Soup
Steak Diane
Soufflé Potatoes
Sliced Tomatoes
Orange Soufflé
Champagne Voisin

Lee Radziwill—full-time princess, part-time actress, and sister of Jacqueline Kennedy Onassis—partook of this interesting and delicious menu at Voisin.

Turtle Soup

1 can turtle soup
1 can beef consommé

Pinch arrowroot, basil, thyme, marjoram, sage, and freshly ground pepper

Mix soups together and bring to a boil. Thicken slightly with arrowroot and add herbs. If possible, add additional turtle meat (diced).

Steak Diane

½ stick butter
1 teaspoon shallots (minced)
1 teaspoon chopped chives
1 tablespoon Sauce Robert
1 tablespoon Escoffier sauce

1 tablespoon Worcestershire sauce
1 teaspoon black pepper
½ inch thick sirloin steak (pounded and flattened to about ¼ inch thick)

This dish is usually prepared at a restaurant table in a large round copper skillet by the captain. However, any skillet will do as well.

Melt butter in skillet and lightly sauté shallots and chives. Pour sauces in pan and add pepper. Place steak in pan and sauté on both sides (a minute or two to a side for rare).

This recipe lends itself to a little originality on your part. Inasmuch as your captain prepares this at your table, the various captains enjoy adding a dash of this or that to make the dish his very own. So if you're out of something in this recipe, it will be just as good—and possibly better—if you add something of your own.

Soufflé Potatoes

Let me warn you right from the beginning that this is not an easy dish for the home cook. Keeping two pots of fat at different, constant temperatures at the same time can undo you. But if you wish to try—good luck.

Pare and slice baking potatoes lengthwise about 1/16 of an inch thick. Soak in ice water until cold. Dry. Deep fry slice by slice, keeping the fat at same hot temperature of about 225°. Shake constantly. The cooking time should be 4 or 5 minutes, and the potatoes will rise to the top. Drain and transfer immediately to another kettle of *very* hot fat (about 425°). The potatoes should begin puffing immediately. Drain on a towel and season with salt.

Sliced Tomatoes

Season only with salt and pepper.

Orange Soufflé

2 cups milk
½ cup sugar
⅓ cup sifted flour
¾ teaspoon salt
½ cup orange juice
3 tablespoons Cointreau
4 eggs (separated)
2 tablespoons butter
2 teaspoons vanilla extract

Grease bottom of 2-quart casserole or soufflé dish. In top of double boiler over simmering water, heat 1½ cups milk until scalded.

Combine sugar, sifted flour, and salt. Gradually stir in remaining ½ cup cold milk and add this mixture to milk in double boiler. Cook over simmering water until thickened, stirring constantly. Add orange juice and Cointreau and continue cooking 5 to 7 minutes, stirring only occasionally.

Meanwhile, beat 4 egg yolks until thick and lemon colored. Stir about 3 tablespoons of double boiler mixture into the beaten yolks. Add yolks to mixture in double boiler and cook 3 to 5 minutes, stirring constantly. Mixture should be rather thick when completed. Remove from heat and blend in 2 tablespoons butter and 2 tablespoons vanilla extract. Set aside.

Beat 4 egg whites until firm. Fold egg yolk mixture into beaten whites and turn into casserole. Place in pan of boiling water and bake at 350° for 1 hour. Serve with sauce.

ORANGE SOUFFLÉ SAUCE

1 pint vanilla ice cream
1 cup whipping cream (whipped)
1 jigger Cointreau

Melt 1 pint vanilla ice cream. Add 1 cup whipped cream and fold in jigger of Cointreau.

Fish à la Veracruzana
Asparagus Mousse
Maian Chocolate Cake
Coffee

The Marquesa de Castellar slept under velvet canopies set with coronets. She promenaded among the two acres of gardens that comprised her estate, the Casa de Piedra in Cuernavaca. But along with this, Rosa de Castellar's life included many checked aprons and many hours spent in her kitchen.

Separated from her husband and unable to maintain her lovely home, Rosa recalled that her friends always said that she served the best table in all Mexico. Accordingly, she let it be known that she would welcome paying guests, and she herself would do the cooking.

Her guest list grew, her fame spread, and the Casa de Piedra became well known for its original and outstanding cuisine. Then, along with all this, romance entered the Marquesa's life and she met and married the attractive Allen Haden, a former newspaperman on the foreign staff of the Chicago *Daily News*.

The day we lunched with them in the beautiful gardens, ex-King Leopold and Princess Lilliane were sitting a few bougainvilleas away, and the dynamic Maria Callas was attracting many eyes.

With so many various dishes to select from for our book, we left it up to Rosa to decide, and she graciously gave us two menus.

Fish à la Veracruzana

½ cup olive oil
4 tablespoons vinegar
2 onions (sliced)
3 tomatoes (cut in quarters)
12 stuffed olives (sliced)
1 green pepper (seeded and
   cut in strips)

1 tablespoon capers
1 clove garlic
1 cup white wine
2 pounds fish filets
Salt, pepper, parsley, oregano
   (to taste)

After preparing the vegetables, pour the olive oil and vinegar into a heavy saucepan. Add the onions, tomatoes, olives, pepper, capers, garlic, and ½ cup of wine. Cook until this reduces a little (about 5 minutes). Now add fish, salt, pepper, parsley, and oregano and the remaining ½ cup wine. Cook until fish flakes easily with fork. Serve with rice.

Asparagus Mousse

2 tablespoons butter
2 tablespoons flour
1 cup milk
1 can cream of asparagus soup
4 eggs (separated)

1 can mushroom soup
¼ cup mushroom caps
Salt, pepper, marjoram
   (to taste)

Make a stiff sauce of butter, flour and hot milk. When ready, thin with a can of cream of asparagus soup and add a few drops of green vegetable coloring.

Add the 4 egg yolks to the mixture. Stir well, but not hard. Beat the whites fairly stiff and fold into the mixture. Pour into well-buttered ring mold. Bake 40 to 45 minutes in a 400° oven, standing in water like any soufflé.

When turned out on serving platter, fill center ring with a mushroom sauce made with mushroom soup, mixed with ½ can milk (or less if you like thicker sauce). Add ¼ cup mushroom caps sliced very thin and season with the spices.

Maian Chocolate Cake

¾ cup sugar	5½ ounces baking chocolate
¾ cup butter	1½ cups ground pecans
6 eggs (separated)	2 tablespoons flour

In an electric mixer at medium speed, beat the sugar and softened butter for 10 minutes. Stop mixer and add 1 egg yolk. Beat 2 minutes. Repeat until all 5 yolks have been used. Melt the chocolate in a double boiler and add. Beat 2 minutes more. Remove bowl from mixer and add the pecans mixed with the flour, using a wooden spoon.

In another bowl beat the 5 egg whites very stiff, using high speed. Fold into the cake mixture.

Butter a round 9 inch deep cake pan and dust the pan lightly with flour. Pour in the cake mixture. Bake at 350° on middle shelf of oven for 35 to 40 minutes. After removing from oven, let cool.

If all this takes up more time than you have, try using a chocolate cake mix and add pecans to it.

ICING

2 tablespoons instant coffee	2 egg yolks
4 tablespoons granulated sugar	½ pint whipping cream
3½ ounces chocolate	

In a saucepan dissolve the instant coffee in ¼ cup of water. Add the sugar and chocolate. Keep on a low fire stirring constantly until chocolate is melted and blended with the sugar. Remove from stove and continue to stir for 5 minutes. Add the egg yolks and mix well. Let cool.

Whip the cream stiff and fold in the chocolate. Put in deep freeze for about 20 minutes. Cover cake thickly with icing and put in freezer for about 3 hours.

Pineapple Omelette with Rum
Zucchini Fritters
Raspberry Meringue Cake
Coffee

The recipe for the raspberry meringue cake came to the former Marquesa de Castellar from the kitchens of the late Czar Nicholas of Russia. It was brought to her by a Russian colonel who sought refuge in France at a time when she was residing in Paris.

Pineapple Omelette with Rum

4 eggs
Small scraping of lemon peel
½ teaspoon salt
2 tablespoons sweet butter

1 small can sliced pineapple
1 tablespoon apricot jam
½ cup rum
1 tablespoon sugar

Beat eggs with scraping of lemon peel, sugar, and salt. Place butter in preheated skillet and add egg mixture. When omelette is half done and becoming solid, chop pineapple into small pieces. Combine with jam and rum and fold into omelette for finishing. Sprinkle with sugar.

Zucchini Fritters

4 zucchini
3 slices thinly sliced sharp
    cheese of your choice

2 tablespoons flour
2 eggs (beaten)
Cooking oil

Cook zucchini in water, being very careful not to overcook as it must be firm. Remove from fire and cut zucchini into fairly thick disks. Between every two disks place a slice of cheese. Dust lightly with flour, roll in beaten eggs, and fry in very hot oil.

⋘ *Raspberry Meringue Cake* ⋙

1 ⅛ cups flour	*1 tablespoon sugar*
Slightly more than ½ cup	*Pinch salt*
butter	*1 ½ ounces Cocoa*

Put flour in bowl. With a wooden spoon, mix in the softened butter, sugar, salt, and chocolate. Lay in 8 inch glass oven dish, covering the bottom and sides as though it were a pie. (It is very crumbly because it is so short.) Put in preheated 300° oven for 15 minutes (the cake should be half cooked when you take it out). Then make meringue (following).

MERINGUE

3 egg whites	*1 teaspoon vanilla*
1 cup sugar	*1 pint fresh raspberries*
½ teaspoon wine vinegar	

With electric mixer, beat the egg whites, sugar, and vinegar for 10 minutes at high speed. Add vanilla and beat another 5 minutes. Fold the cleaned raspberries into the meringue. Fill the half-cooked cake with the meringue and put in oven for another 15 to 20 minutes at 250°.

The original form of this cake used fresh currants, but since they are rarely available in Mexico, the Marquesa substituted raspberries.

Caviar Roses Jacqueline Susann
Other Tidbits
Jellied Madrilene à la Russe
Poached Salmon-Caviar Mousseline Sauce
Head Lettuce with Russian Dressing
Caviar Cake
Champagne

I had invited 250 people to celebrate Jacqueline Susann's latest smash-hit book. Among numerous other items I ordered eight pounds of fresh caviar. Then, remembering that Jackie eats caviar with a spoon (tablespoon), I removed from the deep freeze a ninth pound. I don't expect to rock the cooking world with this information, but yes, you can freeze caviar. The thing to remember, in case it should enter your life, is to let it unfreeze slowly for 24 hours in the refrigerator before using, and *never* refreeze.

As big as the group was, there was no trouble ever locating Jackie for her autograph. "She's next to the caviar," I told everyone who asked.

Naturally, I felt that inasmuch as I was having such a beautiful party for her, she could give me a menu for my book.

"I write, I don't cook," she replied, dashing my hopes.

"But you must have a favorite menu of some kind," I persisted. "And I'll prepare it for you."

She paused a moment, spoon in hand.

"My idea of a dream menu would be caviar with every course."

Well, she asked for it!

I would like to tell you to take this menu with a grain of salt, but I'm afraid you wouldn't be able to down one more grain of anything, much less salt.

When I went into the kitchen after the guests had left, the maids were still cleaning up.

"Can you imagine that group going through nine pounds of caviar?" I asked them.

My own maid replied, "Only eight. It seemed to me you were much too generous with your caviar, so I hid a can behind the soda water in the refrigerator."

I peeked in. The can she saved was the only one that had been frozen.

We were leaving for Greece in the morning so I told the maids, "Have yourselves a drink and eat it up."

Jackie says her French poodle, Josephine, of *Every Night, Josephine* book fame, also loves to eat caviar. She has it on a dog biscuit.

❦ *Caviar Roses Jacqueline Susann* ❦

Wash radishes and remove roots. Cut off top quarter. Pare thin slices of each radish, stopping short of the stem. Refrigerate in ice water until red opens into petals. Pat dry. Cut small hole in center of radish and fill with caviar.

❦ *Other Tidbits* ❦

1. Fill small artichoke hearts with caviar.
2. Cut hard-boiled eggs lengthwise. Remove yolks and blend with sour cream to moisten. Season caviar with chives and a few drops of lemon juice. Fill egg halves one-quarter full of caviar mixture. Swirl egg yolks around top.
3. Chop ripe olives very fine. Mix with caviar and capers. Spread on thin slice of smoked salmon or sturgeon and roll in cornucopia shape.
4. Spread caviar on small squares of buttered toast. Sprinkle with lemon juice, grated fresh pineapple, and grated cocoanut.

❧ Jellied Madrilene à la Russe ❧

Fill bouillon cups with canned jellied madrilene. Top with sour cream and a spoon of red caviar.

❧ Poached Salmon-Caviar Mousseline ❧

1 salmon (2-2½ lb.)
White wine
Black peppers

Bay leaf
Chopped parsley

Place salmon in large frying pan in half water and half white wine to just barely cover. Add a few whole black peppers, a bay leaf and a little chopped parsley. Bring to boil. Reduce heat and simmer, covered, until fish flakes easily (10 to 15 minutes). Remove with slotted spatula and drain. Remove skin and place on warm dish. Serve with sauce.

CAVIAR MOUSSELINE SAUCE

1 cup hollandaise sauce
½ cup whipped cream

1 tablespoon black caviar

Place hollandaise sauce in bowl and fold in whipped cream. Lace through with black caviar.

❧ Head Lettuce with Russian Dressing ❧

1 head lettuce
2 cups mayonnaise
1 cup chili sauce

1 teaspoon Worcestershire
sauce
1 cup whipped cream
1 ounce pressed caviar

Wash lettuce. Cut in quarters and refrigerate for crispness. Combine mayonnaise, chili sauce, and Worcestershire sauce. Fold in whipped cream and caviar. Spoon over lettuce.

❧ Caviar Cake ❧

½ pound cream cheese
Sour cream
Juice of ¼ lemon

1 ounce pressed caviar
1 ounce red caviar

Blend cream cheese with enough sour cream to moisten. Add lemon juice. Stir in pressed caviar. Gently pat out mixture so that it is flat and about ½ inch thick. Using a cookie cutter, press out a round shape. Use smaller cookie cutter for next round and place on top of first. You'll probably need a bottle top for the third layer. Refrigerate. When ready to serve, decorate by dotting with grains of red caviar.

Beef Roulades
Noodles with Caraway
Succotash
Graham Cracker Sandwich Delight
Coffee

The man now called Earl Wilson Jr. was once a little boy who rather testily answered to the name "Slugger." In every way the greatest of sons, he was nevertheless the most frustrating of eaters to a mother who loved to cook and a doting grandmother who loved to cook even more.

"Don't worry about me, Mom," the little angel would tell me. "Just steak and mashed potatoes—or hamburgers and French fries —I don't care which."

My mother—who lived with us until she passed away—and I did worry. Could he live on such limited fare? And *we* were getting pretty tired of the same meals. We could not get him to change.

One time, when the parents of a boy friend invited him to dinner in a restaurant, I said to him before he left, "Please don't order steak, Slugger. It's so expensive in a restaurant." He assured me he would not.

When he returned home I said, "Tell me, Slugger, did you order steak?"

"No, Mom," he replied. "I remembered. I ordered filet mignon instead."

Then he met a beautiful girl named Susan Bauer, and more and more frequently he was away from home for dinner. One afternoon Susan innocently told us, "We're having Slugger's favorite meal tonight—beef roulades."

I laughed, but it was no laughing matter to the adoring grandmother, who was furious. From that time on whenever I would come home and ask where Slugger was, she would reply coldly, "He's having dinner at *that* house *again*."

Slugger and Susan married, and guess what he's eating now? Steak and mashed potatoes or hamburgers and French fries.

What some boys won't do to win a girl!

And so I give you what for a short time was Earl Wilson Jr.'s favorite dinner.

❧ *Beef Roulades* ❧

4 slices round steak (about ¼ pound each)
Butter

Mustard
Cornstarch or flour
Salt, pepper

Pound steaks to make them softer and thinner. Spread each one with a little butter and mustard. Roll up each slice and fasten with skewer or tie with string.

Place side by side in skillet and brown on all sides. When browned, add boiling water to almost cover. Cover and let come to a boil. Lower heat and simmer on top of stove for about 2 hours, adding more boiling water if needed. Remove roulades and thicken water with either cornstarch or flour. (Smooth flour or cornstarch with a little cold water before adding, and have roulade's water boiling.) Season to taste.

Mrs. Bauer, Susan's mother, relates that her mother used to add a little sour cream at the end, instead of thickening with cornstarch or flour. She also says that Germans put a slice of thin bacon and a slice of dill pickle on top of each roulade before rolling.

❧ Noodles with Caraway ❧

8 ounces noodles
Butter or margarine

Caraway seeds
Salt, pepper

Cook noodles as directed on package. Drain and add butter or margarine. Salt and pepper to taste, and sprinkle caraway seeds all through.

❧ Succotash ❧

10 ears corn
1 quart fresh green lima beans
1 slice salt pork

Salt, pepper
½ cup light cream

Cut corn off cob. Boil beans, pork, and 3 corn cobs in salted water for half an hour. Drain beans. Combine corn with beans and add seasonings and cream. Cook in double boiler for half hour.

Frozen or canned vegetables may also be used. Simply heat together. Drain and add the cream and seasonings and let cook until cream becomes incorporated with vegetables.

❧ Graham Cracker Sandwich Delight ❧

8 graham crackers
Butter
½ pint whipping cream

1 pint berries (lightly
stewed)

Butter and toast graham crackers in oven. Whip cream until stiff, and combine with any lightly stewed berries (canned or frozen may be used as well). Be sure all fruit is drained before using. Place fruit mixture on one cracker and top with another cracker.

Irish Cottage Pie
Scallions and Radishes
Fresh Blueberries
Irish Coffee

On a visit to Dublin, we drove to the Ardmore Studios, where fascinating Peter O'Toole was filming his latest picture. It was one of the most attractive and unusual studios we had ever seen. Situated in Bray County, Wicklow, it was just a shower away from Dublin. Ireland is green because it has an annual thirty inches of rain in the lowlands and from forty to sixty inches in the mountainous regions.

The studio had a separate bar and commissary. (Hollywood studios provide a commissary but *never* a bar.) The room was decorated in what looked like driftwood, with deep leather chairs surrounding the tables.

Sitting there with Peter, we all had a simple and delicious dish that he had recommended. Of course, having lunch with Peter could make any dish delicious, but Irish Cottage Pie stands on its own.

Whatever you eat in Ireland should be followed by Irish Coffee. Peter O'Toole had to miss that final touch of the lunch to rush back to the film set, but before departing he had a couple of cold Irish lagers—and they are nice too.

The Irish scenery is so lovely, the food so excellent, that the studio is building an adjacent motel as a tourist attraction. Maybe you can make it there someday.

Irish Cottage Pie

3 tablespoons bacon fat
1 medium onion (finely chopped)
2 tablespoons celery (finely chopped)

2 pounds ground round steak
Salt, pepper (to taste)
Pinch monosodium glutamate
Mashed potatoes (seasoned)

In bacon fat in large skillet sauté onion and celery. Season meat and strew around skillet. Use fork to lift and toss meat in pan until it is evenly cooked and thoroughly mingled with the onion and celery. Place meat in casserole dish and cover entirely with mashed potatoes. Twirl potatoes with spoon so they form peaks. Place in 350° oven until warmed through. Put under broiler to brown peaks.

Use juice in skillet to make a pan gravy and serve over all.

Irish Coffee

Use large Irish goblets. Place 2 tablespoons brown sugar in bottom of each. Fill goblets with very strong hot coffee and a large jigger of Irish whiskey. Stir until sugar is dissolved. Whip cream until heavy but not stiff. Gently float about ½ inch of cream on top of coffee.

Clam and Tomato Broth
Beef Wellington
Artichokes with Swanson Sauce Hollandaise
Clos de Vougeot Burgundy 1959
Bibb Lettuce with Mustard Dressing
Chocolate Mousse Almondine
Espresso
Pear Brandy

W. Clarke Swanson Jr. comes by his gourmet tendencies very naturally. His father, his uncle Gilbert, and his grandfather Carl spent years in the study and preparation of fine food to bring to the table the now famous TV dinner.

What finally became an instant success started out as an instant failure. The chickens looked beautiful and they were tender—but they were also tasteless. Grandfather Carl, who had been a successful raiser of chickens, was chagrined. He used the finest, but something was wrong.

However, the Swanson men were very resourceful. In the matter of good food they knew exactly where to go for advice—home.

They all agreed that Grandmother Swanson's chickens were always tasty and delicious. The following morning they brought her to their large, beautiful, and costly kitchens. She gazed with astonishment as she saw the so-called "food experts" skinning the chickens prior to cooking, and throwing away the skins.

"Don't you know," she said, "you can't get any taste from a chicken without the skin? That's where the flavor comes from!"

They heeded her advice, and the result is history.

Now young Clarke, in the cable TV, radio, and newspaper business, is carrying the Swanson name to even greater heights. His inborn sense of good food has produced this menu, which his wife, Elizabeth, has frequently served, both at their Florida residence and their duplex pied-à-terre in New York.

❧ Clam and Tomato Broth ❧

1 can clam juice	Celery salt
1 can tomato bouillon	Black pepper
Worcestershire sauce (a dash to a cup)	½ pint whipped cream

Combine equal parts clam and tomato bouillon. Season to taste and heat. Serve with salted whipped cream floating on top.

❧ Beef Wellington ❧

Prepare pastry dough first.

4 cups flour	8 tablespoons vegetable shortening
1 teaspoon salt	1 whole egg (lightly beaten)
¼ pound butter	8 tablespoons cold water (about)
½ teaspoon sugar	

Run fingers under cold water, and with tips of fingers blend together in chilled mixing bowl the flour, salt, butter, sugar, and vegetable shortening. Dough should be handled as little as possible. When mixed, add the egg and drip in the water a few drops at a time. Mix until all ingredients are blended through. Wrap in waxed paper and chill in refrigerator. (A pie crust mix may be substituted.)

Prepare filet to be wrapped in the crust.

2 pounds filet of beef
½ cup red wine
Salt, lemon pepper (to taste)
⅛ pound sweet butter
4 tablespoons vegetable
  shortening

4 strips bacon
8-ounce tin liver paté
2 tablespoons chopped truffles
  or chopped ripe olives
1 egg (beaten)

Marinate beef in wine for 2 hours, turning occasionally. Fry bacon until crisp. Drain and put to one side. Dry beef with towel. Season meat with salt and lemon pepper and brown on all sides in the bacon fat.

Preheat oven to 450° for at least 10 minutes. Pour off excess bacon fat from pan and add butter and vegetable shortening to pan. Place meat in pan in oven.

The complaint of many, especially men, is that Beef Wellington is never rare enough. For very rare, roast for only 10 minutes, ordinary rare about 15 minutes, and 20 minutes for medium. Turn meat in the fat half way through roasting. Remove meat from pan and place on dish to cool to room temperature before proceeding. Reserve pan fats and juices to make gravy later. This will be fairly dark in color.

Crumble bacon very fine into paté, add truffles or olives, and spread thickly all around meat.

Roll out pastry into rectangular shape about ⅛ inch thick. Place filet top down in the middle of the dough. Fold each end to form triangle and fold over top as though you were wrapping a package. Brush seams with one lightly beaten egg to seal, and then again lightly over tops and sides. Transfer to *greased* baking sheet, seam side down. Place in preheated 425° oven and bake until pastry is golden brown on top (about 35 minutes).

MUSHROOM SAUCE

1½ tablespoons flour
1 bouillon cube dissolved in
  1 cup water

Fats and juices from pan
Button mushrooms
½ jigger sherry (about)

Dissolve flour completely in bouillon. Scrape pan of drippings and pour bouillon into the fats and meat juices. Stir over medium flame until gravy is desired thickness. Add mushrooms and sherry and stir until mushrooms have warmed.

✖❦❧ *Artichokes with Swanson Sauce* ✖❦❧ *Hollandaise*

Wash artichokes and with a scissors cut spiky ends from leaves. Cut stem off base. Cook in boiling salted water to which has been added 1 tablespoon lemon juice and 1 tablespoon oil until a leaf can be pulled off easily (depending on size, 20 to 35 minutes). Remove choke when artichoke has slightly cooled (it will fall apart if too hot).

SWANSON SAUCE HOLLANDAISE

¼ *pound butter*	*Juice of* ½ *lemon*
½ level *teaspoon flour*	¼ *teaspoon salt*
3 *tablespoons cold water*	3 *egg yolks*

Begin to melt butter in saucepan over lowest flame possible. Dissolve flour completely in water, lemon juice, and salt. Pour into egg yolks and beat until yolks are thick and lemony color. Pour into melting butter and stir vigorously—still on very low flame— just until mixture begins to thicken (about 30 seconds). Lift saucepan above flame about ½ inch and stir until it thickens slightly more (about 1 minute). Then lift saucepan about 4 inches above flame and stir vigorously until sauce is desired thickness and is very creamy and smooth (about 2 to 3 minutes). Will make 1 cup and will never curdle.

For a delicious mustard hollandaise, add Gulden's prepared mustard to taste to the finished hollandaise.

Bibb Lettuce with Mustard Dressing

Wash lettuce and put in bowl of cold water in refrigerator to crisp.

Add ½ teaspoon powdered mustard and a pinch of sugar to French dressing. Let marinate with a clove of garlic for ½ hour. Remove garlic and marinate lettuce in dressing.

Chocolate Mousse Almondine

½ pound Maillards sweet
  chocolate
4 tablespoons sugar
4 egg yolks
4 tablespoons milk

1 tablespoon vanilla
Pinch salt
1 pint whipping cream
Toasted almond slivers

Melt chocolate in double boiler. Add sugar, egg yolks, and milk that have been beaten together. Cook until medium thick. Add vanilla and salt. Cool. Whip cream until stiff and fold into the chocolate. Spoon almond slivers through chocolate mixture, reserving a few to sprinkle on top when ready to serve. Refrigerate for several hours.

Salad Niçoise
Paupiettes de Veau Niçoise
Rice
French Wine (Côte de Provence)
Brie Cheese
Ice Cream
Fruit

Cinderella found her Prince only through the help of a fairy godmother who rescued her from a life of drudgery with her cruel stepmother and jealous half-sisters. But truth can be more exciting than fiction. Grace Kelly was queen of our silver screen. She was surrounded with family, love, respect, and wealth when she met the Prince who won her heart over all the other glamorous suitors.

Her wedding was the talk of the world. More than 1,000 reporters came to carry the story to an adoring populace. It was all the fairy tales come true.

There was no way to accommodate all the press, and many had to be content with stories they picked up at bars. At one point all the American press received a beautiful formal invitation for a reception. Miss Kelly would receive them at the Palace at eight o'clock. The foreign press received nothing. The American reporters surreptitiously displayed their invitations, which drove the foreign press wild. Miss Kelly, of course, could not make herself available to all reporters.

Using every means of subterfuge at their disposal, the foreign reporters also appeared at eight o'clock, only to find that Miss Kelly was Mary Kelly, a member of the NBC press and no relation whatsoever, and the Palace was the Palace Hotel.

The Americans had conceived this joke while sitting around wondering what to do, and they hugely enjoyed the discomfiture of the foreign press, who had sent them off on a few goose chases, too. After a few drinks the foreign press enjoyed it as well, although they missed out on seeing the *real* Miss Kelly and partaking of the elaborate wedding dishes that were provided for the famous guests. One of those dishes has become a Palace favorite and is often served to family and friends in the Palace garden.

Now, some fifteen years later, Her Serene Highness Princess Grace de Monaco has sent us this delightful luncheon menu so that we may all enjoy it.

Salad Niçoise

1 head Boston lettuce
6 hearts of endive (sliced crossways)
12 pimento olives (sliced in half)
2 tomatoes (quartered)

6 rolled anchovies (sliced)
3 strips prosciutto ham (sliced)
French dressing
Gruyère cheese (grated)

Serve with French dressing to which a little garlic salt has been added, and freshly grated pepper. Mix salad ingredients and sprinkle grated Gruyère cheese over all.

Paupiettes de Veau Niçoise

4 veal scallops (about ¼ pound each)
Pepper, salt
4 ounces sausage meat

2 ounces button mushrooms (chopped)
½ cup spinach (chopped)
Pinch of basil and oregano

½ small onion (chopped fine)
1 small clove garlic
  (crushed fine)
1 whole beaten egg (use only
  enough to bind)
4 strips bacon
1 tablespoon butter

1 tablespoon cooking oil
¼ cup white wine
1 cup chopped tomatoes or
  strained canned tomatoes
1 cup chicken consommé
12 pitted ripe olives

Veal scallops should preferably be cut from the filet. Place scallops on a board and pound until thin. Season with salt and pepper.

Mix the sausage meat with the chopped mushrooms, spinach, herbs, chopped onions, and garlic. Bind together with beaten egg. Season with salt and pepper.

Put about a tablespoon of this stuffing in center of each scallop and fold the veal in four. Cover with fine strips of bacon and tie up with string.

Melt butter and cooking oil in a shallow pan and gently fry the paupiettes till light brown all over. Strain off all the fat. Add white wine to pan, plus tomatoes and consommé. Simmer for about 1 hour. When cooked, add black olives and simmer 1 minute longer so olives are warm. Check seasonings.

If desired, paupiettes may be taken from pan and placed under broiler for a minute or two to dry out bacon. Then remove from broiler and carefully cut off strings. Place on warm platter and pour sauce over them.

The Palace allows two paupiettes per person, but this is a lot for luncheon unless you have big eaters.

R&R Oysters à la Rockefeller en Casserole
Orange and Onion Salad
Maraschino Cherry Ice Cream
Café Brulot-Brennans

Gourmets flock in droves to the renowned Brennan's restaurant in New Orleans (and now Houston and Dallas, Texas). One of its many dishes of note is Oysters Rockefeller. That's a classy, classic combination of spinach, oysters, and various other ingredients all served on the half shell. (You'll find that fresh oysters complete with shells are not always available, but oysters by the pint, or frozen, or canned are usually obtainable.)

Because this dish is so delicious, so healthy, and nutritious, we set to work, added a bit of this and that, changed it a little, and put it in a casserole for family meals.

We were so happy with our innovation that, having met Happy (Mrs. Nelson) Rockefeller on several occasions, we thought it would be great fun to name our dish "Happy Oysters Rockefeller." So we wrote to her.

Our happiness was short-lived. Our request was denied, because Mrs. Rockefeller "gets so many requests that she only lends her name to organizations preparing cookbooks for the benefit of established agencies"—nor would she approve the use of her name.

So we just took both our first initials and named it after ourselves. Anyhow we tried, and we think our concoction is almost as delicious as Rockefeller money—at least to eat. Ever try to bite a dime?

R&R Oysters à la Rockefeller en Casserole

½ cup flour
2 cups melted butter
1 cup beef consommé
½ teaspoon salt
¼ teaspoon cayenne
½ cup finely chopped parsley
1½ cups finely chopped spinach

1 cup minced onions
¼ cup minced anchovies
1 tablespoon anise flavoring
2 cups bread crumbs
1 clove minced garlic
2 dozen oysters (about)

Stir sifted flour into 1 cup melted butter. Do not brown flour. Blend in consommé, salt, and cayenne and slightly thicken. Stir in parsley, spinach, onions, and anchovies. Simmer covered for 20 minutes. Remove cover. Stir in anise and cook until thickened.

In another pan, brown bread crumbs in remaining 1 cup melted butter to which minced garlic has been added. (Use more garlic if you wish.)

Butter casserole dish and place layer of greens, layer of oysters, and layer of bread crumbs. Repeat with another layer. Bake in preheated 400° oven for about 5 minutes.

Orange and Onion Salad

2 onions (sliced thin)
Milk
Orange sections

Romaine lettuce
French dressing

Slice onions and soak in milk in refrigerator for 1 hour. Drain and place orange sections and onions on lettuce. Serve with French dressing.

Maraschino Cherry Ice Cream

1 small jar Maraschino cherries
1 tablespoon brandy

1 pint vanilla ice cream

Slice cherries in half and marinate in brandy for half an hour. Let ice cream soften just enough to combine cherries into it. Chill or refreeze ice cream, depending on how soon you are going to use it.

We believe this to be another R&R recipe, but with all the devoted housewives, mothers, and cooks all looking to please someone with their recipes, to think that *we* are the only ones who ever thought of this would be foolish. All we can say is that we don't *know* of it.

❧§❧ Café Brulot-Brennans ❧§❧

1 cinnamon stick (4 inches)
12 whole cloves
Peel of 2 oranges (cut in thin slivers)
Peel of 2 lemons (cut in thin slivers)

6 sugar lumps
8 ounces brandy
2 ounces curaçao
1 quart strong coffee

In a brulot bowl or chafing dish, mash cinnamon, cloves, orange peel, lemon peel, and sugar lumps with ladle. Add brandy and curaçao, and stir together. Carefully ignite brandy and mix until sugar is dissolved. Gradually add black coffee and continue mixing until flame flickers out. Serve hot in brulot cups or demitasse. This is enough for 10 to 12 cups.

Boiled Ham and Vegetables Edie
Onion-Baked Potatoes
Fruit Dream
Coffee

We were invited to Edie Adams Mills' house in Beverly Hills for dinner one night when her husband, Marty, hastily changed the plans. We were going to a restaurant.

"You see," he explained, "Edie is a venturesome cook—but unfortunately not a good one. She'll throw anything into what she's preparing. Last night topped everything. She made what I refer to as 'Heartburn Delight.' It started out as a meat loaf. She was out of bread so she reached up and threw in some Sugar Pops. Then to make up for the sweetness, she added a little tomato paste and several dashes of Tabasco sauce.

Fortunately, she put it in the oven and forgot about it until it had shrunken to one-tenth the size. Believe me one bite was enough."

We invited them to our house when they were in New York. Knowing Edie's penchant for tossing things into a recipe, I concocted this boiled ham dish for her on which she could hardly go wrong no matter what she threw in. It came out great and she wanted the recipe. I gave it to her, along with extra packages of the spices and herbs I had used just to be on the safe side.

❧❧❧ *Boiled Ham and Vegetables Edie* ❧❧❧

2 to 3 pound smoked ham
    butt
Cider vinegar
Box pickling spice
Dry English mustard
1 bay leaf

1 clove garlic
1 head cabbage
1 bunch carrots
Lemon juice
Salt, pepper, dill

Rub ham all over with dry mustard. Place in kettle and cover with half vinegar and half water. Toss in pickling spice, bay leaf and garlic. Cover and simmer over low fire for three hours.

Wash cabbage. Trim off part of core and cut into quarters. Wash and pare carrots and cut in half. Place cabbage with carrots on top in kettle of boiling salted water. Turn fire down and simmer for half an hour or until vegetables are tender. Drain and turn out on warm platter. Cover with melted butter to which salt, pepper, a squeeze of lemon juice, and a sprinkling of dill has been added.

❧❧❧ *Onion Baked Potatoes* ❧❧❧

4 baking potatoes
Cooking oil
4 pats butter

½ package onion soup mix
Sour cream

Wash potatoes and rub with cooking oil. Bake in 350° oven for 1 hour or until tender when pricked with a fork. Remove potatoes from oven and slice off top one-half inch with sharp knife. Scoop out potato and mash with butter. Mix just enough sour cream into the onion soup mix to bind together. Combine with the potato and restuff the shells. Bake for another 20 minutes.

❧❧❧ *Fruit Dream* ❧❧❧

Any fresh or canned fruit
1 pint sour cream
Dark brown sugar

Combine any fruit you desire with sour cream. (If fruit is canned, drain first.) Place in either casserole dish or individual ramekins. Cover entirely and thickly with brown sugar (about a one-quarter inch thickness). Place under broiler turned high and let stay until sugar melts and begins to caramelize (from 3 to 5 minutes). Serve.

Soupe à l'Oignon Gratinee
Poularde Pavillon
Endive and Watercress Salad
Rocher Hericard
Coffee

Le Pavillon at Park Avenue and East 57th Street in New York City is one of the most glitteringly social restaurants, a favorite of gourmets and also of the better-to-do entertainment personalities, including Ed Sullivan.

Ed has had the most successful show format TV has ever known, with over twenty years of Sunday night shows. He searches the world for good acts and performers, and then never intrudes on them. His wife, Sylvia, is a perfect partner for him, with her dry sense of humor. An evening with them is always a delight.

Not long ago we dined with them at Le Pavillon and they ordered Poularde Pavillon. Inasmuch as Sylvia eats no white meat and Ed eats no dark, this is one of their favorite dishes. To paraphrase Jack Sprat:

> Ed could eat no dark and Sylvia could eat no white.
> So when dining on Poularde Pavillon,
> they could eat down to the very last bite.

❦ Soupe à l'Oignon Gratinée ❦

2 medium onions (sliced thin)	2 10¾-ounce cans beef
1 tablespoon butter	consommé
Salt, pepper, paprika (to taste)	Small loaf French bread
Dash Worcestershire sauce	Parmesan cheese

Slice onions thin and brown in butter. Season delicately with salt, pepper, paprika, and Worcestershire sauce. Add consommé and simmer, covered for 20 minutes.

Cut French bread crosswise, quite thin, and toast. Sprinkle Parmesan cheese on each slice and dot with butter. Pour soup into oven-proof bowls. Place toast slices on top of soup and brown under the broiler.

❦ Poularde Pavillon ❦

3-pound chicken	3 shallots (chopped fine)
1 teaspoon salt	4 mushrooms
4 tablespoons butter	1 sprig parsley (chopped)
Dry French champagne	2 bay leaves
4 cups heavy cream	Pinch of thyme

Preheat oven to moderate (350°). Season chicken with salt. Truss it and place in a small casserole with 2 tablespoons butter and 2 cups champagne. Bake about 45 minutes. Baste every eight minutes and turn until the chicken is an even golden brown on all sides. Cut off string, and keep chicken warm on hot platter.

SAUCE

Add to juices in the casserole the cream, shallots, mushrooms crushed by rolling with a bottle, parsley, bay leaves, and thyme. Simmer on top of stove until sauce has reduced to two-thirds the original amount. Strain through a fine sieve into a clean saucepan.

Place over medium heat and swirl in 2 tablespoons butter. Add 6 ounces champagne. Spoon some of the sauce over the chicken, and serve the rest separately.

At Le Pavillon the chicken is brought to the table whole and is carved by the captain.

⋖⋚⋗ Endive and Watercress Salad ⋖⋚⋗

Wash and separate endive into individual leaves. Wash and cut off long stems of watercress. Place watercress on top of leaves and serve with French dressing.

⋖⋚⋗ Rocher Hericard ⋖⋚⋗

1 pint lemon sherbet
Spun sugar or store-bought
  cotton candy

Fresh strawberries
1 tablespoon cassis

Stuart Levin, head of Le Pavillon, recommends that no one but a top chef attempt spun sugar, which is made by bringing the sugar to a boil and "then beating it through the air with a whip." When Mr. Levin serves this dessert at home, he makes this all unnecessary by using cotton candy instead.

Place a scoop of lemon sherbet in a sherbet glass. Cover with cotton candy. Top with strawberries that have been marinated in cassis.

French Fried Sauerkraut Balls
Sauerbraten
Mashed-Potato Pancakes
Ohio Tomato Creole
Wilted Cucumbers
Liederkranz
Coffee

Ohio, especially the Cleveland area, is the greenhouse salad bowl of the United States. It has 400 acres of salad vegetable production under glass, and annually produces about 75 tons *per acre* of greenhouse.

It is also known as a Little Switzerland because of its fast-growing reputation for its outstanding Swiss cheese. And although many people think that Liederkranz is an imported cheese, it is actually made in only one place in the world—at the Borden plant in Van Wert, Ohio.

It was discovered quite by accident when, in the early 1920s, a young Swiss cheesemaker named Emil Frey was trying to duplicate the German cheese, Bismarck Schlosskaese, which spoiled in transport.

At that time Frey was making Swiss cheese in upstate New York. The "tasters" of this cheese Frey was trying to duplicate were members of Liederkranz Hall, a famous club composed solely of members of German descent. Frey never did duplicate the cheese they all desired because the members voted this even better.

And so it was named Liederkranz, which translated means "wreath of songs." In 1926 the Borden Company bought out the Monroe Company which was producing Liederkranz and it is now solely an Ohio product.

If I sound like a member of the Ohio Chamber of Commerce— I am not. But I *am* biased, because Ohio and all those wonderful vegetables and cheese nourished my strong, healthy, and energetic Earl, who was born there. God bless Ohio.

We have Al Gerhart, biggie greenhouse salad grower, to thank for this German menu, which his wife, Gerry, has cooked many times for their family and their many friends of German descent.

᷒᷒ *French Fried Sauerkraut Balls* ᷒᷒

¼ *pound cooked ham*
¼ *pound cooked corned beef*
¼ *pound raw bulk pork*
   sausage
1 *cup flour*
½ *teaspoon salt*

½ *teaspoon dry mustard*
1 *cup milk*
⅓ *cup onions (very finely*
   chopped)
1 *pound canned sauerkraut*

Grind ham and corned beef through fine grinder. Add onions. Fry sausage in heavy skillet over medium heat until lightly browned, breaking it into small pieces as it cooks. Add ground ham and corned beef and continue cooking until heated. Sift flour, salt, and mustard together. Add all at once to meat mixture, stirring constantly to combine ingredients. Add milk while stirring. Continue cooking and stirring for 2 to 5 minutes until mixture thickens and flour cooks into mixture. Remove from heat. Add drained sauerkraut that has been finely chopped, and mix well. Chill several hours or overnight.

Shape chilled mixture into balls a little smaller than the size of a walnut. Dip into flour to coat lightly. Then dip into egg batter (beat 1 egg with ⅔ cup milk and ¾ teaspoon salt) and drain. Roll in fine bread crumbs. Fry in deep fat at 360° for 1½ minutes. Drain on absorbent paper and serve hot.

This recipe will make about 75 balls, but they may be frozen and kept till needed.

❦ Sauerbraten ❦

3-pound pot roast (larded)
1½ cup vinegar
½ cup red wine
1 cup water
2 tablespoons sugar
1 teaspoon whole black
    peppers
1 bay leaf
2 onions (sliced)
6 cloves

1 teaspoon dry mustard
3 teaspoons salt
2 tablespoons flour
Dash black pepper
Dash nutmeg
2 tablespoons butter or
    cooking oil
¼ cup light cream
½ cup seedless raisins

Place meat in glass or earthenware container. Pour boiling vinegar, wine, and water over meat. Add sugar, whole peppers, bay leaf, 1 onion, cloves, mustard, nutmeg, and 1 teaspoon salt. Cover and let stand in cool place one or two days, depending on how sour you wish the meat. Turn frequently.

Dry meat well before proceeding. Strain marinade liquid. Combine 1 tablespoon flour, 2 teaspoons salt, and dash of black pepper and coat meat on all sides.

Brown 1 onion in butter or cooking oil in Dutch oven or heavy skillet, not iron. Brown meat on all sides. Add ½ cup marinade. Cover and simmer very slowly 3 to 4 hours or until meat is fork tender, adding more marinade if needed.

Blend 1 tablespoon flour with cream and add to skillet. Add raisins and stir over heat until gravy is thickened.

❦ Ohio Tomato Creole ❦

2 cups diced fresh tomatoes
½ cup diced fresh green
    pepper
1½ cups uncooked fresh corn,
    cut off cob
¼ cup boiling water

1 tablespoon chopped onion
2 teaspoons salt
1 tablespoon butter
⅛ teaspoon black pepper
1 teaspoon sugar

Combine first 5 ingredients in saucepan. Cook until vegetables are tender (about 10 minutes) and mixture has thickened. Add remaining ingredients.

✒️❀ Wilted Cucumbers ✒️❀

1 large cucumber
1 cup onion rings
2 tablespoons oil
1 tablespoon cider vinegar

1 teaspoon salt
¼ teaspoon sugar
Dash fresh pepper

Pare cucumber and cut into crosswise slices ⅛ inch thick. Let stand in salted ice water one hour. Drain and press dry. Combine with onions, oil, vinegar, and seasonings.

✒️❀ Mashed-Potato Pancakes ✒️❀

2 cups seasoned mashed
  potatoes
¾ cup white flour

1 small grated onion
1 whole egg

Mix flour and grated onion with potato. Add beaten egg and beat all together until smooth. Form into pancake-like shape. Fry in a skillet, using bacon drippings, until brown on both sides.

Sugar Baked Ham
Marshmallow Baked Sweet Potatoes
Fruit Salad
Baked Alaska Pie
Tea

Hope Hampton is often referred to as the Duchess of Park Avenue, for that is where she resides in almost regal splendor in a beautiful French-chateau type town house that is the scene of elegant parties.

The former star of stage and screen had been the only starlet to continue to Grand Opera fame. She sang not only in the United States but at La Scala in Rome and at the Opera Comique in Paris. A rich woman, she donated her salary to charity. For this she was decorated by the French government.

All of this seems rather awe-inspiring until you meet Hope. The first things you notice about her are her beautiful iridescent teeth and her charming smile. She swears on a stack of bank books she's never had a filling, much less a cap. That is astonishing when you realize she "practically lives"—all five foot three, 108 pounds of her—on sweets.

Breakfast frequently begins with a large pot of tea and—a big chocolate cake. There is always a box of candy or a bunch of candy bars at hand, and as for ice cream, "never less than three helpings."

A favorite Duchess of Park Avenue dinner menu, which she gave us, consists of some of the sweets (or sweetness) of which she is so fond.

⋖ईई⋗ Sugar Baked Ham ⋖ईई⋗

8- to 10-pound baking ham
3 tablespoons brown sugar
  (heaping)
1 teaspoon dry English
  mustard

1 level tablespoon flour
Pineapple slices
Maraschino cherries

Place ham in a large kettle of water; bring to a boil and let ham simmer for one hour. Cool. If there is a skin on, remove. Mix together sugar, mustard, and flour and spread over ham. Put in 325° oven long enough to brown (about 1 hour). Baste 2 or 3 times during baking. When ham is finished, place slices of pineapple with a Maraschino cherry in center all over top and let warm through.

⋖ईई⋗ Marshmallow Baked Sweet Potatoes ⋖ईई⋗

8 sweet potatoes or yams
Milk or cream
Dash nutmeg
Dash cinnamon
2 tablespoons brown sugar

1 sweet apple (sliced)
1 tablespoon chopped walnuts
⅛ pound butter
1 package marshmallows

Canned sweet potatoes are usually more uniform in color than fresh. If using fresh, boil for 30 to 35 minutes or until tender. Peel and mash with milk or cream. Beat with potato masher until fluffy.

Place layer of potatoes in bottom of buttered casserole dish. Sprinkle with nutmeg, cinnamon, and sugar. Place thinly sliced apples and walnuts over this and dot with butter. Repeat with another layer. Place in 325° oven for about half an hour. Cover top with marshmallows and put back in oven until marshmallows soften and become golden on top.

❧ Fruit Salad ❧

Assorted fruit in season
2 tablespoons shredded
  cocoanut

½ cup whipped cream
1 cup mayonnaise
3 tablespoons fruit juices

Arrange fruits on salad plate and sprinkle cocoanut on top. Fold whipped cream into mayonnaise and lace through with any one or combination of fruit juices.

❧ Baked Alaska Pie ❧

Place layer of strawberry and layer of pistachio ice cream in cooked pie shell. Cover entire top thickly with meringue, making peaks of the meringue. Place under broiler just long enough for peaks to turn golden (a minute or so).

Fatta Omar Sharif
Rice
Endive Salad
Wine
Guava with Cream Cheese

It is the nature of Omar Sharif to be top rank in anything he undertakes. Leading ladies vie with each other to play opposite him—and frequently fall in love with him in the process. However, none of them can be sure that his deep concentration in the love scenes comes from their inspiration—or his working out a bridge problem.

Omar Sharif is one of the top-ranking bridge players of the world and has competed in world championships as a member of the Egyptian team. He has been quoted as saying, "I would rather be a bad actor than a bad bridge player."

His passionate interest in the game has prompted him to assemble Europe's most outstanding bridge players into a single unit known as Omar Sharif's Bridge Circus. Stancraft Products sponsored a tour of the United States and also put out a line of bridge accessories with his picture on the cards. If that wouldn't be enough to throw a girl off her game!

Part of his expertise comes from his great ability to figure percentages. When he enters a gambling casino to play blackjack, croupiers cringe. So, girls, if you want to make time with Omar, you'd better make points.

Fatta is an Egyptian dish he frequently prepares for bridge foursomes when they're playing at his house. But don't for one moment get the idea that Omar keeps jumping up from the table to see how the Fatta is coming along. He prepares what he can ahead of time, and when the game starts the cook takes over. As for guava, either the fresh or the preserved variety, he is so fond of it that he frequently has it for breakfast. As a dessert, he adds cream cheese. He not only loves the flavor of the guava, he enjoys the texture. Wouldn't you know? Whatever he does is exciting.

We can give you the dinner. The best we can do about Omar is to suggest the playing cards with his picture.

⊷§§⊷ *Fatta Omar Sharif* ⊷§§⊷

½ *leg lamb with bone in (about 4 pounds)*
Small yellow onion (peeled)
1 stick cinnamon
½ *teaspoon cardamom seeds (crushed)*
Salt, pepper (to taste)
½ *cup sweet butter*
1 pint goat's milk or yogurt

1 egg
1 clove garlic (peeled)
½ *teaspoon dried mint flakes*
1 cup long-grain rice
4 slices white bread (toasted and diced or crumbled)
3 teaspoons pine nuts (optional)

Trim off excess fat and outer layer of skin from lamb. Cut meat into bite-size pieces. Place bone and meat in pot with enough water to cover, along with whole onion, cinnamon stick, cardamom seeds, and 1 teaspoon salt. Bring to a boil, then reduce heat so meat simmers slowly. Cook 45 minutes (or until meat is tender), skimming at frequent intervals. Remove from stove. Discard bone, onion, and spices. Strain and reserve stock.

Brown lamb bits in about 1½ teaspoons butter. Season with salt and freshly ground pepper to taste.

Mix goat's milk (or yogurt) with beaten egg. Heat until mixture begins to boil (if yogurt, be careful that it does not curdle). Set aside. Heat whole garlic in 1 teaspoon butter with ½ teaspoon salt and mint flakes; remove garlic and discard. Add this garlic butter and yogurt or milk mixture to browned lamb. Meanwhile, cook rice in 2½ cups lamb broth until fluffy.

Place toasted bread (diced or crumbled) in bottom of deep platter or casserole. Top with hot cooked rice. Spoon lamb mixture and sauce over it. Decorate with butter-browned pine nuts. Serve at once.

These proportions will serve 6 to 8.

⊷§⊱ *Endive Salad* ⊷§⊱

Allow two stalks of endive per person. Wash and dry. Remove any bruised outer leaves and cut small slice from base of stalk. Cut in half lengthwise and cover with French dressing to which a goodly amount of freshly ground pepper has been added.

⊷§⊱ *Guava with Cream Cheese* ⊷§⊱

Use fresh guava when available. Preserved guava is referred to as guava shells in the stores.

Serve cream cheese, separately, with toasted crackers.

Gazpacho "21"
Rock Cornish Hen Pot Pie
Romaine and Beet Salad
Vin Louis Martini
Crêpes Soufflès "21" with Sauce Grand Marnier
Espresso

It is said that Singapore is the crossroads of the world. But for many of today's rich, some of whom own their own countries, the crossroads is the "21" Club at 21 West 52d Street in New York City.

Customers of the place, when away from their address books, will write their friends there, knowing that sometime during the week they will drop in. Literally, the women customers are kissed into the place from the front door to their table by Mac, Bob, Pete, Charlie, Jerry, Sheldon—all members of the large Kriendler and Berns clan who operate "21."

You must admit that's a lot better than being "kissed off!"

❧ Gazpacho "21" ❧

1 cucumber
½ pint tomato juice
½ pint stewed tomatoes
½ green pepper (remove
  seeds and dice)
¼ large onion (diced)
1 stalk celery (diced)
½ clove garlic

⅛ cup white wine vinegar
⅛ cup lemon juice
⅛ cup olive oil
⅛ cup chopped pimento
¼ teaspoon Tabasco sauce
Dash Lea & Perrins sauce
⅛ cup parsley (chopped)
Salt, pepper (to taste)

Clean vegetables thoroughly. Place all ingredients in blender for 10 to 15 seconds. Chill and serve. Garnish with chopped green peppers, onions, cucumber. Will serve 4 or 5.

❧ Romaine and Beet Salad ❧

Romaine lettuce
Beets

1 hard-boiled egg (chopped)
French dressing

Clean lettuce thoroughly and crisp. Lay a heaping tablespoon of canned diced beets on top and sprinkle with chopped hard-boiled egg. Serve with French dressing.

❧ Rock Cornish Hen Pot Pie ❧

4 Rock Cornish hens
Cooking oil
¾ cup carrots (diced)
¾ cup onions
¾ cup celery
¾ teaspoon rosemary
2 bay leaves
1½ teaspoons flour
¾ cup white wine
1½ pints brown sauce
  (or chicken broth)

Salt, pepper (to taste)
Dash Lea & Perrins sauce
¾ cup pearl onions
¾ cup baby carrots
¾ cup sliced mushrooms
  (or button mushrooms)
¾ cup peas
¾ cup tiny round potatoes
  (use round scoop)

Clean hens and tie. Roast 15 to 20 minutes at 450°, basting with oil. Add diced carrots, onions, celery, rosemary, and bay leaves. Bake an additional 15 to 20 minutes. Remove birds and cool. In pan where birds were cooked, add to the juice and vegetables the flour, wine, and brown sauce (or chicken broth). Cook over low heat for 15 minutes. Strain. Season with salt and pepper to taste and Lea & Perrins sauce. Set aside.

Split the hens and remove the bones. Place the meat in a casserole. Sauté pearl onions, baby carrots, mushrooms, peas, round potatoes, in butter until cooked. Add these vegetables and the strained sauce to the casserole. Cover top with pie crust.

PIE CRUST

¾ pound all-purpose flour
½ pound shortening
Scant ½ pint cold water

1½ teaspoons sugar
Scant teaspoon salt
1 egg

Cut in shortening with the flour. Gradually add the cold water with the sugar and salt until fairly stiff dough is reached. Let stand a couple of hours in refrigerator. Roll out dough and place on top of casserole. Brush top with beaten egg. Cook at 450° for approximately 20 minutes or until golden.

❧ Crêpes Soufflés "21" with Sauce ❧ Grand Marnier

2 eggs
¾ cup sifted flour
1 teaspoon sugar

Pinch salt
Milk
Cooking oil

Beat eggs. Mix with flour, sugar, and salt. Add milk until batter is consistency of cream. Beat until smooth. Heat 6-inch skillet that has been oiled. Pour 2 tablespoons batter into pan, tilting quickly to distribute batter evenly. Cook until golden brown on one side, then turn and brown other side. Oil pan again and repeat. Keep cakes warm.

FILLING

3 generous tablespoons butter	½ cup sugar
1½ tablespoons flour	1 teaspoon vanilla
1 cup milk	4 beaten egg yolks
3 pinches salt	5 egg whites beaten stiff

Melt butter in a saucepan and mix with flour. Gradually add milk and salt. Stir constantly. Add sugar with vanilla. When sauce is thick and smooth, remove from flame. Add beaten egg yolks and beat all ingredients well. Now add stiffly beaten egg whites. The sauce should be thick and smooth. Let this cool.

Roll filling in the crêpes and place them in semideep casserole. Put casserole in a flat pan with hot water and bake in 400° oven for 15 minutes. Then reduce heat to 375° and bake for an addition 20 to 25 minutes.

SAUCE

1 teaspoon vanilla	2 or 3 pinches salt
1 cup milk	4 ounces Grand Marnier
4 egg yolks	Slivered almonds
¾ cup sugar	Powdered sugar
1 cup heavy cream	Brandy

Add vanilla to milk and scald. Beat egg yolks until light, and add ¾ cup sugar while beating. Gradually add cream and the scalded milk. Add salt. Beat vigorously until well blended. Cook this over a pan of hot water, then remove from flame and add Grand Marnier. Mix again until contents are well blended.

When crêpes are cooked, remove from oven. Sprinkle a generous helping of almonds over top and dust with powdered sugar. Flambé with brandy. Serve immediately with sauce on the side.

THANKSGIVING DINNER
AT THE WILSONS

Turkey
Pan Stuffing
Mashed Potatoes
Mashed Rutabagas
Fried Corn
Cranberry-Orange Relish
Cole Slaw
Olives, Celery, Radishes, Green Onions
Frozen Pumpkin Pie
Coffee

WHEN THANKSGIVING TIME rolled around, Mother and I were always so busy shopping and preparing that you'd have thought we'd been commissioned by the Army instead of just cooking for ourselves and an aunt and two or three friends who might be in New York alone.

I always felt Mother cooked much too much, but if I dared suggest that she would be insulted. There was no such thing as too much—only not enough. Her idea of a groaning board was to have her guests stagger from the table groaning and fall asleep for an hour. Only then was she convinced she had prepared the right amount. If I were to say, "Mother, do you think this is a well-balanced meal?," her reply would always be, "On Thanksgiving you don't have to balance."

One item I always left to her—the turkey. For years I was convinced that Mother's turkey had to be better than mine because it always smelled so much better as it cooked. The aroma of her turkey would permeate the house. With mine—nothing. When I would ask her what I did that was wrong, she would merely shrug.

And it was not until the Thanksgiving before she passed away, when she wasn't well enough to do all that cooking, that she said to me, "Rosemary, when you put the turkey in the oven, sprinkle a little sage all over the top. It doesn't do a thing for the turkey, but it sure makes it smell awfully good."

❧ *Turkey* ❧

*1 14-15-pound oven ready
turkey
Salt and pepper*

*Butter or margarine
Sage*

Season turkey inside and out with salt and pepper. Rub all over generously with butter or margarine. Sprinkle lightly with sage.

Place in 400° oven until turkey begins to brown. Turn oven down to 250° and bake about 3 hours longer. Baste frequently. To test for doneness, move drumstick up and down. If it moves easily and fleshy part of drumstick feels soft to pressure, turkey is cooked.

❧ *Pan Stuffing* ❧

*Loaf of stale bread
2 medium green peppers
    (diced)
½ cup celery (diced)*

*½ cup large onion (diced)
Butter (1 teaspoon)
Generous pinch sage
Salt, pepper (to taste)*

Tear bread apart and put in colander. Run cold water over it. Let drip dry while you cook vegetables in large frying pan in butter until they are soft but not brown. Stir often. Press water out of bread and mix with vegetables in frying pan. Add sage, salt, and pepper.

Siphon off just enough juices from roasting pan to make gravy later. Put stuffing into remaining juices of roaster and mix like a salad. Bake 20 minutes to half hour with turkey. It should be a little brown on top and not soggy. Serve as a side dish.

✐✐ Mashed Rutabagas ✐✐

Pare rutabagas and cut into thin slices. Place in boiling salted water and cook, covered, until tender (about 25 minutes). Drain and mash with butter, pinch of sugar, and salt and pepper to taste.

✐✐ Fried Corn ✐✐

¼ pound bacon (cut in
   quarter pieces)
2 large cans niblet corn
   (drained)

1 teaspoon sugar
Milk

Fry bacon until crisp. Add corn and sugar. Slightly brown corn, then pour milk over all to just cover. Let cook until corn absorbs all milk (about 5 minutes).

✐✐ Cranberry-Orange Relish ✐✐

2 cups fresh cranberries
4 oranges (seeds removed)

4 cups sugar
1 cup chopped walnuts

Put cranberries and oranges, including the rind, through the coarse blade of a food chopper. Stir in sugar. Add walnuts and chill. Makes about 2 quarts.

❧❧ Cole Slaw ❧❧

1 medium cabbage
2 tablespoons cider vinegar
Salt, pepper (to taste)
2 teaspoons sugar

2 tablespoons cold water
½ cup mayonnaise
1 large onion (grated)

Grate cabbage. Mix vinegar with salt, pepper, sugar, and water. Add slowly to mayonnaise. Taste for seasoning. Combine with cabbage and onions. Chill.

❧❧ Frozen Pumpkin Pie ❧❧

1 teaspoon nutmeg, ginger,
  cinnamon (combined)
2 tablespoons hot water
16 marshmallows
2 cups pumpkin
4 tablespoons orange juice

½ cup brown sugar (to which
  has been added pinch salt)
6 eggs (separated)
½ pint whipping cream
2 tablespoons sugar

Soak spices in the hot water. Melt marshmallows in double boiler. Add pumpkin, spices, orange juice, and brown sugar. Mix well. Add beaten egg yolks and beat together until blended. Let cool, then put in freezing compartment until mixture just begins to freeze. Remove and fold in cream that has been whipped stiff. Put back in freezing compartment for freezing. When ready to serve, put in baked pie shell. Top with stiffly beaten egg whites to which 2 tablespoons sugar has been added. Place under broiler until peaks turn golden.

Sweet Rolls à la Chaplin
English Smoked Tea

Just because a man turns 80 is no reason for him to have lost his taste for girls—or other dishes.

Charlie Chaplin made me think of this one sunny summer afternoon at his home outside Vevey, Switzerland. We were discussing food, in which he has a vast interest, and his inordinate pride in his kitchen and the culinary talents of his wife, Oona O'Neill. He certainly has not forgotten girls, for after seeing Sophia Loren in a low-necked gown a few seasons ago, he exclaimed, "Oh, to be 70 again!" Oona is reported to have sighed that she would have liked to be 70 also. They had daughter Annie along about the time that Chaplin was 71, and a son, Christie, when he was 75ish.

The high point of our visit was the butler's summons to tea. Although it was a sweltering afternoon in the Alps to us, our soft-voiced, round-faced, little genius host found it chilly and hauled from the closet a caracul-collared coat and even wanted us to cloak ourselves for the stroll across the beautiful 37 acres. He warmed his back against the burning logs in the fireplace and remarked, "I hope to go to Hell when I die so I can keep warm."

We had trod the lawn stretching in front of the "White House" type residence all the way to the pool, with the snow-peaked Alps in the distance, and possibly we were ready for a bit of sustenance when the butler announced tea.

Charlie Chaplin definitely inquired whether we would like a whisky or vodka, and just as we were about to say "What an excellent thought," he mischievously said, "My old lady"—Oona—"never lets me have a drink before 6." Whereupon we smiled widely over the "tea," realizing that our dreams of a drink had been dashed because it was barely 4:30.

While the tea was being poured and Mr. Chaplin's caracul coat was going back in the closet, I helped myself to one of the sweet rolls presented by the butler.

"Ohh, my!" My bite was too large or misdirected, for the roll and the plate it was on hit the floor. My husband, observing this mishap, was about to rebuke me, at least with a scowl if not with words, when his sweet roll and his plate also slapped the floor.

"What will Mr. Chaplin think of us?" I was thinking, when Mr. Chaplin's plate and his sweet roll plunked on the carpet.

The butler swept up the residue neatly in his hands and a napkin and passed us replacements.

Then, our hands now sticky from the two helpings of sweet rolls, we followed Mr. Chaplin to the kitchen where he introduced us to his cook and bragged at length about his wife Oona making better fish soup than the famous French chefs' bouillabaisse.

As we were leaving leisurely by limousine a half hour later, with Mr. Chaplin ever so graciously shaking hands and wishing us well, I had a sudden thought: Did he drop his roll on that beautiful carpet deliberately to keep us from being uncomfortable because we'd dropped ours? We'll never know.

❧ *Sweet Rolls à la Chaplin* ❧

Oona was ill in bed that day and I didn't wish to disturb the household for the sweet roll recipe as I thought I could manage to duplicate them when I got home. So, while this recipe may not be theirs, the rolls look and taste the same—and are just as hot.

2 packages Pillsbury's crescent
   dinner rolls
16 ounces tart red pie cherries
2½ tablespoons cornstarch
½ cup sugar

⅛ teaspoon salt
1 teaspoon butter
1 teaspoon lemon juice
1 egg

The crescent rolls come eight to a package and are in triangles. Place 2 triangles together and make one square by pinching seams together.

The filling directions were on the can of cherries for a pie. I used these directions but added an extra ½ tablespoon cornstarch. Cook until thick, stirring constantly. Let get very cool. Put about 1 tablespoon of filling in middle of dough and roll. Pinch ends together and shape slightly, if you wish. Brush beaten egg over top. Bake at 375° until golden brown. (Mine took about 20 minutes, although the directions gave a shorter time.) When finished, remove from oven and brush with butter and sprinkle with sugar.

Sandy's Monster Salad
Steak Teriyaki
Wild Rice
Rosé Wine—Mistral
Frozen Berries over Ice Cream
Coffee

At fourteen, Sandy Dennis was already stagestruck. When at seventeen she starred in *The Rainmaker* with the Lincoln Community Theater in Lincoln, Nebr., where she lived, that settled it. With her parents permission and $100, she headed for New York.

Her star was in its ascendancy, although she didn't realize it. One day, flat broke, she was window shopping in Greenwich Village. A fellow stopped her and asked her if she was an actress. He turned out to be an Off-Broadway director, and she got into an Ibsen revival. From then on it was a few steps to Broadway and Hollywood. Sandy gathered awards along the way—even Moscow Film Festival's Best Actress Award, the first time the honor had been given to a non-Russian.

She set up housekeeping in Hollywood with her three cats and two pooches of dubious pedigree, to start work in *Who's Afraid of Virginia Woolf?* Then she met and married jazz saxophonist and composer Gerry Mulligan.

Now in a rambling country house in Connecticut, she can enjoy all the things she loves—animals, old movies, wild flowers, books, and good food that she prepares, despite her insistence that she hates to cook. In fact, the reason this is her favorite menu is that she claims it requires little skill and little preparation.

We think Sandy is underestimating herself. She should have some sort of an award for even dreaming it up.

❧ Sandy's Monster Salad ❧

(Sandy says she has not specified amounts in her salad because it all depends on what vegetables you would like to have the most of.)

Fresh spinach leaves
Endive, whole leaves
Cherry tomatoes
Green pepper (sliced thinly)
Capers
1 cucumber (thinly sliced)
Sliced pimento
Red onion (sliced paper-thin)
Minced garlic clove (used to
    rub bowl before adding
    ingredients)

Oregano
Celery seed
Carrots (sliced)
Artichoke hearts
Green olives
Black olives
Mashed hard-boiled egg
Feta cheese (crumbled)
Olive oil
Vinegar

❧ Steak Teriyaki ❧

1½ pounds flank steak (this will feed two amply, but when buying for more, allow for considerable shrinkage)

MARINADE

¼ cup soy sauce
¼ cup honey
¾ cup vegetable oil
2 teaspoons ground ginger
⅓ cup white raisins (soaked
    and drained)
Small can water chestnuts
    (sliced)

½ green pepper (diced)
Small can mandarin oranges
    (drained)
⅓ cup chopped onion
Small can pineapple (drained
    and crushed)
2 tablespoons vinegar
1 large clove garlic (minced)

Combine all marinade ingredients. Marinate meat overnight, if possible, without refrigeration, or at least six hours.

Drain meat and place on barbecue rack or on broiler near flame. It is a thin cut and will take approximately 6 minutes on each side for a pink center.

Reserve marinade, draining off oil from top as much as possible. Pour into saucepan and heat over a low flame. Serve as a sauce for meat, or over the wild rice.

⋘ Frozen Berries over Ice Cream ⋙

Defrost berries and pour over ice cream as a sauce.

Eggs au Foie Gras
Sole in Aspic
Mediterranean Rice Salad
Fruited Grapefruit
Coffee

No individual broadcast newsman has been seen by more people (twenty million each night), nor covered more major stories, nor reported on a greater variety of subjects than CBS News Correspondent Walter Cronkite in his eighteen years with CBS. His record as a journalist, reporter, foreign correspondent, and commentator extends for thirty years. He has covered coronations, participated as a United Press correspondent in the first B-17 air raid mission during World War II, landed with the invading Allied troops in North Africa, taken part in the Normandy beachhead assault after which he dropped with the 101st Airborne Division in Holland, and accompanied the U.S. Third Army in the Battle of the Bulge. And so it continued through the years, including visiting South Vietnam.

I'm sure many of us, sitting eating dinner and watching television, have wondered when he ever gets time to eat with his lovely wife, Mary (Betsy to her friends) and their three children, Nancy Elizabeth, Mary Kathleen, and Walter III. And as for entertaining, how did his wife ever manage?

I posed this question to Betsy and it made her laugh. Everyone knows that Walter must be at the station well in advance, and if anyone believes he can say goodnight to the audience and rush home—they're mistaken. Frequently there are well-wishers, and often an important guest who wants to talk a while after the show is over. So, a long time ago, Betsy sized up the situation. When she has guests she serves a buffet that can stand for hours if need be, and if her guests choose to go ahead, there's always plenty of food and it's just as good when Walter arrives. You will see just how delicious and simple all these things are when you try them. Thanks a lot, Betsy.

Eggs au Foie Gras

8 ounces pâté de foie gras
or liver pâté
1 tablespoon sour cream

8 hard-boiled eggs (halved)
Slivers of truffle or chopped
ripe olive

Moisten pâté with sour cream. Remove yolks from eggs and mash with pâté, adding more sour cream if necessary to make smooth. Add truffles or olives. Stuff whites with mixture by heaping spoonfuls. Refrigerate.

Sole in Aspic

1 package unflavored gelatin
½ cup cold water
2 12-ounce cans consommé
madrilene
⅛ teaspoon salt

2 jiggers sherry wine
8 poached filets of sole
16 canned asparagus tips
1 tablespoon capers

Soak gelatin in cold water to soften. Add to salted consommé. Bring to a boil and immediately remove from flame. Let cool slightly and add sherry.

Place filets in shallow dish. Lay asparagus spears around fish and sprinkle with capers. Pour consommé over all and refrigerate until set.

❧ Mediterranean Rice Salad ❧

2 cups packaged precooked
  rice
½ teaspoon salt
1½ cups chilled cooked peas

1 cup sliced pimento
1 cup diced tomato
French dressing with garlic
  added

Cook rice as directed on package. Refrigerate. Marinate peas, pimento, tomato and salt in French dressing and refrigerate. When ready to serve, combine all and place on lettuce leaves.

❧ Fruited Grapefruit ❧

Marinate melon balls, seedless grapes, and grapefruit sections in a little sugar and champagne (white wine may be substituted) for half an hour. Chill slightly. Serve in hollowed grapefruit shells and top with mint leaves. More wine may be added if desired.

Cold Cucumber Soup
Chili con Carne
Toasted Tortillas
Mexican Beer
Peppermint Stick Ice Cream

Trini Lopez, born Trinidad Lopez III, lived as a child with his parents and five brothers and sisters in a one-room house in Dallas, Texas. Theirs was a poverty-ridden existence.

At the age of eleven Trini formed a small combo along with other eleven years olds and developed a crowd-pleasing singing style to lure small change from the passersby. At fifteen he was singing in nightclubs. He was still not able to make ends meet when he got a three-month engagement to sing at P.J.'s in Hollywood. It was there that Don Costa saw him for the first time and spoke to Frank Sinatra about him. Sinatra signed him to an exclusive contract with his record company, Reprise Records. Less than a year later, Trini was well on the way to making his first million.

The first thing he did was to buy his parents a big home in Dallas. He no sooner did, than he had screams of protest—the neighbors were complaining because Trini's father wanted a truck garden in the exclusive neighborhood. The tall corn growing above the fence was considered very unsightly.

"So I bought 'em another lot, bigger and with a higher fence, and every day my Dad came back with big baskets of food and fruit," Trini says.

At Trini's first engagement at the Riviera in Las Vegas, he sent for his parents and got them ringside seats at his opening. Engaged with last minute rehearsals, he had them met by Tony Zoppi, the publicity man, at the airport. Tony was surprised to see Mrs. Lopez carrying so many shopping bags and bundles, but he refrained from commenting.

Arriving at the hotel, Mrs. Lopez requested the use of the kitchen. Despite the kitchen being crowded with cooks preparing all the food for a sold-out opening night, they made room for her. And there she placidly prepared Trini's favorite dish of Chili con Carne and Toasted Tortillas, the ingredients for which she had brought with her in the bags and bundles.

A much sought-after bachelor, Trini says he has no fixed idea of the kind of girl he will eventually marry. "It just has to be the right chemistry, something in the stars."

In the meantime, he will continue to pursue his favorite hobby, women.

"I love people," Trini confesses. "And especially girl people."

⋙ Cold Cucumber Soup ⋙

2 10¾-ounce cans cream of
celery soup
2 cups cream
¾ teaspoon salt
⅛ teaspoon ground pepper
2 cups diced cucumbers
⅓ cup chopped onion
Paprika

Heat soup and cream to which salt and pepper have been added. Refrigerate. When cold and ready to serve, stir in combined cucumbers and onions. Top with slice of cucumber and a dash of paprika.

❧ Chili con Carne ❧

3 pounds ground chuck or
    hamburger
1 large green pepper
1 large onion
2½ teaspoons salt
4 tablespoons cooking oil
6 tablespoons Masa Harina or
    flour
2 tablespoons chili powder

2 cloves fresh garlic or
    1¼ level teaspoons garlic
    powder
1 tablespoon whole ground
    comino or 1¼ teaspoons
    comino powder
1¼ teaspoons oregano
3 cups beef stock
7 cups water

Place meat in water in cooking utensil. Add green pepper, onion, and 2 teaspoons salt. Cook 30 minutes over medium heat. Drain meat, saving stock. Remove pepper and onion.

Add cooking oil to cooking utensil and when hot, add meat, breaking meat during frying process. Cook about 5 minutes over medium heat. Add Masa Harina or flour and dissolve with meat. Add chili powder, stirring at all times. Add spices and remaining ½ teaspoon salt. Remove fat that forms on top of beef stock. Measure 3 cups and add to meat.

Cook for 30 minutes, stirring from time to time. Yields about 6 servings.

If beans are desired, add 3 cups cooked pinto or red beans (drained). Cook another 30 minutes (total cooking time 1½ hours). With beans, yield is about 9 servings.

❧ Toasted Tortillas ❧

The canned or packaged tortillas are as excellent as you could make. Serve either plain toasted or add a thin slice of cheese and then an even thinner slice of hot Mexican pepper before toasting.

❧ Peppermint Stick Ice Cream ❧

Smash peppermint sticks with a hammer between two paper towels. Add to softened ice cream and refreeze.

⌘ *Chili con Carne Strictly B.W.* ⌘

We would like to add our own recipe for Chili con Carne. Everyone who has tasted it likes it and eats enough of it to be convincing.

We do not start from scratch, but take advantage of the prepared foods available to give us lucky housewives a real good product. And now that we've made that explanation, here we go with Texas in hot pursuit.

6 strips bacon
1 teaspoon paprika
1 teaspoon chili powder
½ teaspoon black pepper
¼ cup minced onions

½ teaspoon salt
1 pound ground round steak
2 cans Chili con Carne with
beans

Cook bacon until crisp. Remove and drain on paper. Sprinkle paprika, chili powder, and pepper in fat and sauté onions. Salt meat and cook in same pan, breaking apart meat as you go along.

Empty canned chili into large kettle. After meat is cooked add to kettle, including all juices. Crumble bacon through. Taste. If not hot enough, add more chili powder and stir through. Before serving, simmer on a low fire until all is thoroughly heated.

Chili is better if made the day before so everything marinates.

Minestrone with Garlic Bread
Linguine with White Clam Sauce
Salad with Roquefort Dressing
Dry White Wine
Melon Balls with Anise
Coffee

It takes some stars hundreds of light years to make their existence known on earth, but it only took Flip Wilson ten years and five minutes. The ten years were spent working his way up from eighth-rate nightclubs, and the five minutes comprised his debut on the Tonight show. Since then, he's made many appearances on the Ed Sullivan show, and his nightclub engagements read like a roster of the best hotels and clubs in America.

Flip came from crushing poverty and a large family in Newark, N.J. His youth was spent shuttling between foster homes. At sixteen he dropped out of high school and joined the Air Force, where his quick wit earned him the title of "Flip" from his buddies and brought him to the attention of his commanding officer, who tutored him in English and sent him to typing school. He ended his service career on the Pacific outpost lecture circuit, addressing the men on such erudite topics as the cocoanut crab, "who will only mate in the water. If he's seventy-five miles inland, he's going to crawl back to the water to make it—you've got to want to make it pretty bad to do that."

Completing his stint in the service, Flip took a job as a janitor in a San Francisco hotel. One night, at the last minute, Flip was recruited to play a drunk in a hotel show. After that he started

—by hitchhiking—on a tour of night spots where the salary of the performer depends on the generosity of the house. Wherever he went, he took along Max Eastman's *The Enjoyment of Humor* and studied it like the Bible. Now he has written a book of his own comedy rules as a guide to other aspiring comics. He begins with "the first law of humor is that things can be funny only when we are in fun." When you're with Flip, that's the way things are.

What he said about this menu was: "This is my very favorite dinner menu, but if I cooked it myself, I wouldn't eat it—because I can't cook!"

Minestrone with Garlic Bread

Heat two 10-ounce cans of minestrone soup. Top with Parmesan cheese before serving and pass extra cheese for those who wish it. Serve with garlic bread.

Linguine with White Clam Sauce

*1-pound package linguine
(broken into thirds)*
¼ pound butter
2 cloves minced garlic

½ cup parsley (chopped)
*2 cans minced white clams
(do not drain)*

Cook linguine in boiling salted water according to directions on package. Melt butter in saucepan. Add garlic, parsley, and undrained clams. Warm through. Drain linguine and place in individual bowls. Spoon sauce over each.

Salad with Roquefort Dressing

*2 ounces Roquefort cheese
1 cup French dressing*

*1 large head lettuce
(quartered)*

Mash 1 ounce Roquefort cheese into dressing so that dressing is creamy looking. Sprinkle remaining cheese over top. Serve over lettuce.

Melon Balls with Anisette

Assorted melon balls
1 tablespoon powdered sugar
2 tablespoons cold water

2 tablespoons Anisette liqueur
(or anise flavoring)

With rounded scoop form balls of various melons—cantaloupe, Persian, watermelon. Combine sugar, water and Anisette. Let balls refrigerate in marinade for half an hour, turning occasionally. May be topped with sprig of mint if desired.

Essence of Mushroom Soup
Duckling au Poivre
Sautéed Potatoes
Fiddlefern, Baby Squash, Mangetouts
Lemon Sherbet with Strawberries in Cassis
Rose Petal Parfait
Coffee

Exotic tropical trees, overhanging tubs of plants spilling pink phlox and red coxcomb, the ripple of water in a marble pool. Babylon? No. The Four Seasons Restaurant, 99 East 52d Street, New York City.

The vegetables that are presented to you on a beautiful tray in raw form for your selection, to be cooked to order, are among the specialities of the house. As an out-of-town friend said to us one evening, "I've heard of buying diamonds by the carat—but never carrots by the diamond!"

Whenever we dine there we recall an incident that happened back in 1965. Sharman Douglas was hosting a swinging kitchen party there for 237 "intimates" of Princess Margaret and Lord Snowdon. The elite of society along with the elite of the theatrical world were to be there. Roz Russell, Truman Capote, Sammy Davis Jr., Harry Belafonte, Ethel Merman, the John Lindsays— to name hardly any. But the press was barred!

Well, no one can do that to my Earl and get away with it. Disguised as a pantryman, from his tall chef's cap down to his new tennis shoes, plus a French moustache and painted-on side-burns, he got in by presenting a letter identifying himself as an extra pantryman, who was to help out in the kitchen. He had written it himself and signed it "Jean Pierre Gros." Of the many friends he believed detected his disguise, no one blew his "cover." Naturally he had a great column the next day.

Afterward we went there for dinner. Earl ate some of the delectable dishes his mouth was watering for but he had not been able to partake of as "pantryman."

I asked Paul Kovi, director of the Four Seasons, to let me have the recipes for this dinner that Earl selected, and I thought you would enjoy it, too.

ཚེ Essence of Mushroom Soup ཚེ

10 ounces dried mushrooms
   (chopped)
12 ounces fresh mushrooms
   (chopped)

40 ounces chicken consommé
Parmesan sticks

Let dried mushrooms infuse with 12 ounces of the consommé for half an hour. Pour the infusion into the balance of the consommé and add the chopped fresh mushrooms. Cook over low flame until fresh mushrooms are tender. Do not allow to boil.

Serve in consommé cups with Parmesan sticks.

ཚེ Duckling au Poivre ཚེ

One 4- to 5-pound duckling
Monosodium glutamate
Salt
10 ounces black pepper
   (crushed)

2 ounces cognac
2 cups chicken consommé
1 cup light cream

Rub cavity of duckling with a small amount of monosodium glutamate and salt. Place duckling, breast side up, in shallow open pan. Roast at 375° for about 2½ to 3 hours. Duckling is done when fatty portion of leg feels soft when pressed and moves easily up and down. Do not baste.

Fifteen minutes before duck is cooked, remove from oven and spread the pepper over all the duckling. Then put back in oven for the additional time.

Pour off all the fat from the pan. Pour the cognac over the duckling and flame. Remove duckling from the pan. Add the consommé and cream. Strain the sauce and serve separately.

⋞ॐ⋟ Sautéed Potatoes ⋞ॐ⋟

4 Idaho potatoes (peeled and
sliced)

Butter
2 ounces sliced truffle

Brown potatoes in butter. Season to taste and add truffles at last minute.

⋞ॐ⋟ Fiddlefern, Baby Squash, Mangetouts ⋞ॐ⋟

Steam fiddleferns and serve lightly buttered.

Sauté or steam California baby squash and also serve lightly buttered.

Mangetouts, which means "eat all" in French, are the delicate peas in their pods, sometimes called snow peas. They are lightly sautéed in butter and eaten whole.

⋞ॐ⋟ Lemon Sherbet ⋞ॐ⋟

2 cups water
About 2 cups suger

Juice of 8 lemons

Sweeten water with sugar to taste. Add lemon juice and stir thoroughly. Pour mixture into freezing tray and place in freezer. Stir occasionally to prevent separation. Serve with Strawberries in Cassis.

❦ Strawberries in Cassis ❦

10 strawberries   4 ounces sugar
2 ounces Cassis liqueur

Marinate all together for 2 hours.

1 cup heavy cream   ½ pound sugar
12 egg yolks   2 ounces Cassis liqueur

Combine heavy cream, beaten egg yolks, and sugar. Bring to a boil, stirring occasionally. Add Cassis liqueur. Combine this with marinade. Will serve from 4 to 6.

❦ Rose Petal Parfait ❦

4 tablespoons raspberry   8 slices banana
  preserves   Juice of 2 oranges
10 rose petals   2 tablespoons whipped cream
8 dates (chopped)

Divide all ingredients into four parts. Place them in parfait glasses in following order: 1 tablespoon raspberry preserve, 2 rose petals, 2 chopped dates, 2 slices banana, juice of half an orange. Repeat in same order with balance of ingredients. Top with whipped cream and decorate with 1 rose petal. Serves 2.

Peter Pool's Chocolate Marshmallow Pecan Fudge
Mint Fudge with Toasted Almonds
Walnut Caramel Fudge
Sherry Caramel Fudge

IT'S PETER POOL'S MOTHER SPEAKING—RUTH POOL, MY COL-
LABORATOR, HAS THE FLOOR AND THE TYPEWRITER. LISTEN WELL.

Long before Dr. Peter E. Pool worked in his laboratory for heart
research at the University of California at San Diego, he was just a
little boy with a sweet tooth. On a rainy day I would suggest,
"How about making fudge? You can help and then lick the pan."

He would stand at my side and I would ask, "How many cups
of sugar? Cream?" He would dutifully answer, "Two—one."

One day he said, "All my friends are out playing. Do I *have* to
stand over a hot stove helping? Seems to me you ought to be able
to remember yourself by now. After all, you only make two kinds
and you can save the pan for when I come in."

I took his departure graciously. But the "only two kinds"
rankled.

I had been making marshmallow and pecan fudge. No, instead of marshmallow and pecans, I substituted toasted almonds
and added mint flavoring. The caramel fudge I left the same but
added half a jigger of sherry.

"Hey, Mom," he said admiringly when he tasted the new con-
coctions, "I knew you'd come up with some new ideas if you just
tried hard enough."

He knows how to flatter his mother and he often does, but I like to think that a tiny part of his success in research is due to remembering that Mom took an old formula and found a new approach.

Today, away from his busy laboratory, Peter flies a plane, surfs, and sails a catamaran off the sandy beach of La Jolla. Only one thing has changed. While Peter is off "playing," his wife Mary (Mickey) is home cooking the fudge.

⋖§⋗ Peter Pool's Chocolate Marshmallow ⋖§⋗ Pecan Fudge

2 cups white sugar
1 cup sour cream
2 squares unsweetened
   chocolate

½ teaspoon salt
1 teaspoon vanilla extract
1 cup chopped pecans
1 cup miniature marshmallows

In saucepan combine sugar, sour cream, chocolate, and salt. Stir over low heat until sugar dissolves. Then stir occasionally. Test for doneness by dropping small amount of mixture into cold water. When ready to take off fire it will form a soft but firm ball.

Remove from heat and let cool until saucepan feels lukewarm to touch. Add vanilla. Beat with electric beater until fudge forms definite ripples and you can feel it beginning to set. Toss in pecans and marshmallows all at once and give it only one or two extra twirls so that the marshmallows will remain firm and not disintegrate into the fudge. Turn into greased pan. Refrigerate.

⋖§⋗ Mint Fudge with Toasted Almonds ⋖§⋗

Follow same directions as above but omit marshmallows and pecans. Add to recipe 1 teaspoon mint flavoring and toasted almond slivers.

❧ *Walnut Caramel Fudge* ❧

1 cup white sugar
1 cup brown sugar
1 cup coffee cream

1 teaspoon vanilla
1 cup chopped walnuts

Follow cooking directions for chocolate fudge above.

❧ *Sherry Caramel Fudge* ❧

Follow directions and ingredients of caramel fudge but add 1 tablespoon sherry.

Jackie's Baked Mac
Celery and Raw Carrot Strips
Broiled Grapefruit with Honey

When Jackie Gleason comes off one of his severe diets and chalks up a sixty-pound reduction, he sometimes enjoys celebrating by feasting on baked macaroni—"Jackie's Baked Mac" to the Great One.

He will have been following a high protein diet—eggs one day, fish one day, meat one day—and drinking lots of water to "disperse the ash," and he will have been satisfying his sweet tooth by eating desserts made with sugar substitutes or fresh fruit with honey.

Here's Jackie describing to us how to prepare the "mac" and finish it off: "Sprinkle Parmesan cheese across the top and bake it. When it is brown on top, and you are so hungry that you feel like climbing into the stove, it is done. You will, also, have gained 4,000 pounds!"

Jackie's Baked Mac

1 pound macaroni	3 tablespoons milk
Salt	1-pound can stewed tomatoes
1 pound sharp fresh Cheddar cheese	Parmesan cheese

Cook macaroni in boiling salted water according to directions on package. Melt Cheddar cheese with milk in top of double boiler.

Drain tomatoes, making sure all the juice is gone. Mash well with a fork and add to melted cheese. Pour over macaroni and shake so that mixture runs all through. Place in a well-buttered casserole dish, sprinkle with Parmesan cheese, and bake in 350° oven.

⋙ Broiled Grapefruit with Honey ⋘

Slice grapefruit in half and remove core. Loosen sections and pour tablespoon of honey over top. Broil under flame until honey has turned a little brown and the grapefruit is warmed through.

Cocktails
Fresh Vegetables and Clam Dip
Scampi and Garlic Bread
Veal and Peppers
Green Spinach Noodles
Acorn Squash
Green Salad
Pouilly Fuisse Wine 1964
Fresh Fruit Cup
Espresso and Petit Fours
Brandy and After-Dinner Liquers

Carol Lawrence and Robert Goulet have one of those rare successful show-business marriages because they both make every effort to keep their family together in spite of the demands of two separate careers.

They were married in 1963 and are seldom long separated from each other or from their sons, Christopher and Michael. Carol has been known to fly from coast to coast on her day off to spend a day with the children.

She considers herself a wife first, a mother second, and a star third, and she only arranges her appearances after Bob's commitments are firm. She wouldn't sign for *I Do! I Do!* on Broadway until Bob had signed to star in *The Happy Time*, also on Broadway. They then moved the children from their Beverly Hills home and took an apartment in New York and a house in suburban New York where the children could romp.

When Carol says she's a wife first she is serious. She has a passion for decorating and loves to sew. She made the Austrian shades that hang in their New York living room, but more than anything she loves to cook and entertain.

"I mostly use old Italian recipes that take two or three days to make," she told me. "By that time, Bob can't resist the aromas any more, and I have to serve the food."

This menu, which is Bob's favorite meal, is on the agenda weekly in the Goulet household.

⋅⋅⋅ Clam Dip ⋅⋅⋅

1 large package cream cheese
1 can minced clams (drained)
1 pint sour cream
5 large garlic cloves (crushed)

Juice of 1 large lemon
Red cayenne pepper
Tabasco sauce

Have cream cheese at room temperature. Blend in the sour cream & clams. Mix in crushed garlic and lemon juice. Add cayenne pepper to taste and a few drops of Tabasco sauce.

Spoon the dip into a pretty bowl and surround it with fresh vegetables in bite-sized pieces and arranged in the most appealing Japanese manner. Cauliflower florets, carrots, celery, radishes, green peppers and cherry tomatoes are among the vegetables I use.

⋅⋅⋅ Scampi ⋅⋅⋅

Large raw shrimp in shells
    (largest you can find, about
    6 per person)

6 large garlic cloves
    (per 2 pounds of shrimp)
¼ pound butter
Fresh parsley

Shell the shrimp, leaving the tail shell intact, and split them in half lengthwise so they open out like butterflies. Slice garlic cloves in half and brown in butter until they are golden brown. Add shrimp and one whole bunch of parsley, coarsely chopped and dripping wet. Cover tightly and simmer just until the shrimp turns a beautiful pink and the parsley wilts.

Serve immediately with garlic bread (below) and garnish with *more* parsley (to calm any lovers in the group who worry about all that garlic!).

⋅§⋅ Garlic Bread ⋅§⋅

1 large loaf Italian bread
Butter

Crushed garlic
Grated Parmesan cheese

Slice loaf of bread lengthwise as for a huge hero sandwich. Cream butter with crushed garlic and grated Parmesan cheese to taste and spread inside the loaf of bread. Put halves of loaf together and wrap in aluminum foil. Heat in 450° oven for 5 minutes and serve.

⋅§⋅ Veal and Peppers ⋅§⋅

3 medium-size onions
3 green peppers (cut in 2-in. squares)
½ cup butter
½ cup corn oil
Veal cutlets (ask butcher to prepare 4 cutlets as for veal scallopine: very thinly sliced and then pounded flat

between two pieces of paper)
Flour
Sherry or dry white wine
2 cups chicken stock or consommé
Arrowroot
Freshly ground black pepper
Grated Parmesan cheese

Slice onions thinly and separate into rings. Brown onion rings and green peppers in butter and corn oil until tender. Remove and keep warm. Add a little more oil to the skillet and dredge the cutlets in flour, and brown on both sides. Cover cutlets with wine. Cover skillet and simmer over low flame for 3 or 4 minutes, turning the meat so that both sides of each cutlet "drink" the wine.

Add chicken stock and thicken the mixture with a small amount of arrowroot blended with a little cold water. Simmer a few minutes. Sprinkle with black pepper.

Place cutlets in large oven-proof serving dish with cover and pour sauce over top. Add onions and green peppers and sprinkle liberally with Parmesan cheese. Cover and place in 450° oven just until cheese melts.

ৰ৯৯ৰ *Green Spinach Noodles* ৰ৯৯ৰ

Prepare one package of green spinach noodles according to directions. Drain and return to pot. Add butter and Parmesan cheese to taste.

ৰ৯৯ৰ *Acorn Squash* ৰ৯৯ৰ

2 acorn squash (*halved*) Cinnamon
12 tablespoons butter Cloves
12 tablespoons brown sugar

Split the squash in halves (one half per person), remove all seeds, and rinse. Slice a half-inch piece off the rounded side of each half to stabilize them in pan. Place in oven-proof dish with cover. Fill each cavity with 3 tablespoons butter and 3 tablespoons brown sugar. Sprinkle lightly with cinnamon and cloves. Add an inch of water to baking dish (maintain that level of water throughout baking). Bake at 350° to 400° for 1 hour or until absolutely fork tender.

ৰ৯৯ৰ *Green Salad* ৰ৯৯ৰ

"Bob and I happen to adore salads, and I just keep adding and mixing by smell and feel and taste. I use an assortment of lettuces —romaine, iceberg, red leaf, and chicory—with tomatoes, cucumber, a little celery, radishes, carrots sliced in rounds, and one or two avocados. Toss all by *hand* with corn oil, crushed garlic, oregano, sweet basil, fresh parsley, and lemon juice."

"I arrange honeydew and cantaloupe melon balls in the bottom of a champagne glass, then add sliced strawberries, whole raspberries, and in the center a few fresh blueberries topped with a dab of lime sherbet and a sprig of mint. I pour cold Seven-Up over each fruit cup and serve with lots of hot espresso and a plate of petit fours."

Sherry's Mish Mosh
Salad
Coffee

Sherry Britton, one of the most beautiful of all the stripteasers, who's been whistled at since World War II, lives across the street from me. Although quite a dish herself, you would never think she could prepare one. But this beauty whom I see out walking her dog revealed to me an economy meal she invented when she was just married and money was scarce.

Often she had leftovers. In Mish Mosh, she found a delightful solution, because it was such a flexible dish. She could use any meats, tidbits one might otherwise throw out, and leftover gravies.

Graduating to the legitimate stage, the economic situation eased. Now, her many friends, recalling the lean years and having enjoyed this dish with her, occasionally ask her to make it especially for them.

❧ *Sherry's Mish Mosh* ❧

1 cup packaged precooked rice
1 teaspoon chicken bouillon
3 tablespoons butter
2 medium onions (diced)
1 large green pepper (washed, seeded, and cut in 1 inch slices)
2 all-beef frankfurters (sliced ¼ inch thick)

1 cup cooked diced pork
1 cup cooked diced chicken
1 package frozen peas
¼ cup soy sauce
½ cup water
Salt, pepper (to taste)
1 small can mushrooms (optional)

Prepare rice according to directions on box, plus 1 teaspoon chicken bouillon.

Melt butter in Dutch oven or casserole (which you will use later in the oven and then serve from at the table). Sauté onions and green pepper until onions are transparent. Add franks and continue sautéing for about 5 more minutes. (At this point mushrooms may be added, if desired.)

Add pork and chicken, frozen peas, soy sauce, and a ½ cup water. Toss all ingredients lightly, cover, and bake in 375° oven for about 15 minutes, or until peas are tender and water has been absorbed.

Salad

½ head romaine lettuce
2 endives
½ head iceberg lettuce
½ red onion (sliced)
Grated Romano cheese

1 tablespoon oregano
Salt, pepper (to taste)
6 tablespoons olive oil
2 tablespoons wine vinegar
Garlic powder (to taste)

Wash and drain greens and break into bite-size pieces. Put into salad bowl and add onions. Sprinkle grated cheese generously, coating top layer. Add oregano, salt, and pepper. Toss lightly. Add oil and vinegar and garlic. Toss together.

"The High and the Mighty" Martini
"Soldier of Fortune" Venison Stew
"Fiddler's Green" Salad
Floating "Island in the Sky"

Aircraft commander, sailor, and writer Ernest K. Gann is a wanderer in the classic tradition. Built like a middleweight with the cool level eyes of a mariner, he is as fiercely independent as a Tuareg bandit. A perfectionist at many things, he is equally so about food.

When he was sailing a brigantine across the Atlantic, an experience later described in his story, *Soldier of Fortune*, the first person he chose for his crew was a top chef.

Writing was a craft that Gann set out to learn with the same concentration that he brought to celestial navigation and blind flying. As a result, most of his books have been made into pictures. One of his books was copied word for word by a prisoner, who submitted it to a publisher under a new title. It was enthusiastically accepted. Fortunately it was recognized as the work of a plagiarist.

All of his novels are based on personal experiences. The thrilling rescue that takes place in *Island in the Sky* was a rescue that Gann himself made, for which he received a Distinguished Flying Award. When the novel was made into a picture, Gann did the piloting for the spectacular flying into deep ravines—wing tips barely escaping the mountainous sides.

This is a typical Gann menu that either a chef might prepare in the middle of the Atlantic or his wife, Dodie, might serve on their farm in the San Juan Islands, where he works a solid session each day on his next book.

❧ "The High and the Mighty" Martini ❧

Pour 1½ ounces chilled vodka into a chilled martini glass. Add 2 or 3 drops of dry French vermouth and a small pimento olive.

❧ "Soldier of Fortune" Venison Stew ❧

3- to 4-pound venison steak
1 cup olive oil
2 cups dry white wine
2 teaspoons mixed herbs
1 tablespoon whole black peppers
1 clove garlic

Salt and pepper
2 medium onions (sliced)
1 stalk celery (sliced)
1 carrot (pared and thinly sliced)
5 strips bacon (fatty)
½ cup heavy cream

Place venison in earthenware bowl or casserole. Pour over it the olive oil and wine. Add mixed herbs, peppers, and garlic. Cover and let marinate 36 to 48 hours, turning meat now and again.

Reserve marinade. Wipe meat dry, salt and pepper, and brown it on both sides in hot fat. Transfer it to oven-proof dish. In same fat, fry onions, celery, and carrot and add to meat. Strain marinade and heat. Pour over meat. Cover meat with slices of bacon. Roast in covered container about 2 hours at 300°. Remove lid, increase oven to 450°, and cook for 15 minutes more.

Remove meat and keep hot. Take off as much fat as possible from juices. Strain marinade and boil juices down in saucepan on top of stove. Add cream and taste for seasoning.

❧ "Fiddler's Green" Salad ❧

Chicory
Endive
Watercress
Romaine
1 clove garlic

2 teaspoons salt
1 teaspoon freshly ground pepper
1 teaspoon paprika
½ teaspoon sugar (optional)

½ teaspoon powdered
   mustard
Dash of Tabasco sauce
½ teaspoon Worcestershire
   sauce

1 cup olive oil
¼ cup red wine vinegar
2 yolks hard-boiled eggs

Wash greens thoroughly and crisp in refrigerator. Mix dry ingredients together. Blend liquid ingredients. Mix and pour over greens.

❧ Floating "Island in the Sky" ❧

1 quart milk
⅓ cup granulated sugar
¼ teaspoon salt
3 eggs (separated)
4 tablespoons powdered sugar

1 teaspoon cornstarch
1 tablespoon almond flavoring
1 tablespoon sherry
1 tablespoon slivered almonds

Scald milk in large skillet. Add granulated sugar. Remove from flame and cover.

Add salt to egg whites and beat to medium consistency. Gradually add powdered sugar and beat until stiff.

Bring milk back to boiling and drop the egg whites by heaping spoonsful into the milk. Cook for 1 or 2 minutes on both sides or until egg whites have puffed a little. Remove with perforated spoon and drain on dry cloth.

Combine beaten egg yolks with cornstarch in top of double boiler. Gradually stir in milk from pan. Cook over boiling water until mixture thickens. Remove from flame. Cool slightly and add almond flavoring and sherry. Fold in nuts and chill. Serve with egg whites on top of custard.

Pan-Fried Chicken
Roumanian Mamaliga
Tomato Aspic-Sour Cream Dressing
Date and Pecan Pie
Coffee

We had just met Groucho Marx for the first time and were thrilled to make his acquaintance. Groucho had only been married (to his second wife) for a short time, and exclaimed about her fried chicken. We simply must taste it.

"In fact," he said, "we're having a party and she'll serve it. There'll be a lot of celebrities there, and booze and fried chicken. Thursday night at 6 o'clock. Would you come?"

"We sure will!" Earl whipped out pencil and notebook. "What's your address?"

"Wouldn't you like to know!" snapped Groucho.

Of course he did give us the address—and the fried chicken was delicious.

Pan-Fried Chicken

Butter and shortening	Salt and pepper
2 medium sized chickens cut in pieces	4 tablespoons flour

Melt equal amounts butter and shortening together in skillet—about ½ inch deep when melted. Clean chicken under cold water. Shake off water but do not dry as salt and flour sticks better. Rub salt and pepper over chicken. Dredge chicken in flour and drop in hot fat. Brown on both sides, cover for 5 minutes. Then uncover to complete crisping. This should take 10 to 15 minutes each side.

To make gravy, scrape the browned bits from the pan. Blend in a little flour and brown; slowly add milk. Season to taste.

When I fry chicken I always cook a lot extra. As my father used to say, his idea of heaven was to open the ice-box and find a platter of cold fried chicken. Inasmuch as Earl feels the same way I always cook loads of it.

At home we usually have mashed potatoes with this but the Roumanian Mamaliga was delicious with it.

❧ Roumanian Mamaliga ❧

Corn meal
½ pound fresh sharp cheese—
    Cheddar or American

⅛ pound butter
½ pint cream

According to instructions on box, prepare corn meal mush to serve four BUT add one extra cup water.

Divide cooked mush in thirds. Place a layer in bottom of greased casserole dish. Dot liberally with butter and place thin slices of cheese on top. (Do not use a processed cheese as it does not melt as well as fresh.) Sprinkle with a tablespoon of cream. Add another layer of the mush and repeat process for three layers ending with cheese mixture on top. Cover with aluminum foil and place in preheated 350° oven. Bake for forty minutes.

❧ Tomato Aspic-Sour Cream Dressing ❧

2 packages unflavored gelatin
2 12-ounce cans tomato juice
Juice ½ lemon
Worcestershire sauce

1 pint sour cream
1 tablespoon dried dill
Salt, pepper (to taste)

Soak gelatin in cold water to soften. Add to seasoned tomato juice. Let come to a boil and remove from fire. Add Worcestershire. Pour into salad mold and chill until firm. Serve with sour cream to which the dill has been added.

⊷ Date and Pecan Pie ⊷

½ cup butter
½ cup sugar
½ cup light corn syrup
½ cup maple syrup
4 eggs

1 cup chopped pecans
½ cup chopped dates
1 teaspoon vanilla
1 teaspoon bourbon

Work butter until creamy; add sugar, syrups, and eggs (well beaten). Stir in vanilla and bourbon and mix well. Add nuts and dates and pour into 8 inch pie shell and bake one hour in moderate 350° oven.

Spaghetti Israel
Beet and Pineapple Salad
Israeli Melons
Coffee

There is excellent food to be had in beautiful, and at times scorching hot, Israel.

Fifteen years ago Americans sent them food packages, for they were hungry. Today you see "Weight Watchers" signs.

It seemed unusual to us that while many of the restaurants are nonkosher, the big hotels such as the Hilton and Sheraton in Tel Aviv are run on a strictly kosher-kitchen cuisine. Not being greatly familiar with this kind of a diet, we weren't sure what to expect. Certainly we were unprepared for the fabulous buffet breakfasts. On a large circular steel table there was an enormous array of delicious fish, such as herring, sardines, salmon, and sturgeon, plus cream cheese with chopped chives and other delicious fillings, large vegetable salads, and assorted breads and rolls with many kinds of jellies. There were also fresh and stewed fruits, and the fruits in Israel are delicious. You could, of course have eggs in any form, although naturally not with ham or bacon. No one missed it.

We spent most of our time with our good friend, Mira Avrech, who is a leading Israeli columnist. She went to Israel as a little girl from Germany. Still in her teens, she served in the war in Palestine in the underground. She took us to Jaffa and showed us where she had gone into active combat for the first time. Creeping around a building on a reconnaisance mission, she told us, she suddenly came upon the enemy face-to-face—and was forced to shoot and kill two people. This was the experience of many young Israeli girls.

Mira now lives in a beautiful penthouse with a large open living room filled with a profusion of plants growing both indoors and out.

She prepared a supper for several of us and served us delicious spaghetti, along with a colorful and delightful salad and an assortment of Israeli melons. I have tasted melons in many parts of the world, but never any as succulent as these.

I remarked to Mira that I had read in a national magazine of the marvelous chocolate cake that Golda Meir baked. I wished that I could have her recipe, but wouldn't dream of imposing on this very busy woman for it.

Unknown to me, Mira wrote to Mrs. Meir and received a most gracious though surprising letter. Golda Meir wrote that she would have been most happy to have supplied me with her recipe, but unfortunately she didn't have one. She had been cooking many things for many years but—she had never baked a chocolate cake in her life!

Spaghetti Israel

1 large onion
2 large green peppers (cut up)
Olive oil
1 pound ground meat
About 20 green olives
2 large tomatoes
Salt, pepper (to taste)
½ teaspoon rosemary
12 ounces tomato paste
½ cup white wine
About 2 tablespoons dried dill
Spaghetti
Butter
Parmesan cheese

Sauté onion and green peppers in olive oil until golden brown. Add meat and sauté. Add olives and sauté all together. Cut tomatoes into small pieces and sauté. Add salt, pepper, rosemary, tomato paste, and wine. Sprinkle with dill. Cook uncovered until you have a thick sauce. Add more wine, if desired.

Cook spaghetti according to directions. Oil a large bowl with olive oil. Pour spaghetti into sieve and then into oiled bowl. Top richly with butter and mix. Top with considerable amount of Parmesan cheese and mix. Pour sauce on top and mix all together. Serve piping hot.

⋙ *Beet and Pineapple Salad* ⋘

Combine an equal amount of julienne cut beets and chunks of very soft ripe pineapple (canned pineapple chunks may be used). Be sure both are well drained. Make a dressing of equal amounts of mayonnaise and sour cream. Stir well through beets and pineapple. (The dressing will become juicy and pink in color.)

⋙ *Israeli Melons* ⋘

Cream cheese and crackers are frequently served with the melons as an accompaniment.

"Poor Man's" Beef Wellington
Au Gratin Potatoes
Cauliflower with Lemon Parsley Butter
Relish Bowl
Coffee Marshmallow Whip
Coffee

We were on a junket that took us to the opening of the Hilton Hotel in Cairo. The assembled stars of stage and screen included Van Johnson.

On the opening day, Conrad Hilton provided a most lavish and spectacular party in a huge tent in the desert. While those who wished to do so could travel by car, the more adventurous were put on camels and horses. Fortunately, we went by car, and just made the tent in time to avoid a sandstorm. Those who came by camel and horseback were somewhat disheveled on arrival.

The tent was magnificently decorated, and we had Egyptian music and belly dancers. One of the most lavish buffets I have ever seen was laid out for the guests to enjoy after cocktails.

The knowledgeable people there assured us that these sandstorms were always of very short duration. This one fooled them—it was long, it was violent, and many of the guests were nervous. It was Van with his exuberance and talent who became the "hero of the Hilton" and saved the party. Jumping up on one of the big tables, Van sang and did belly dances with the professionals, and soon had everybody laughing and applauding, forgetting the increasing violence outside. Finally it did subside. The princely buffet supper, however, was a complete disaster—it was entirely covered by about half an inch of sand!

Van, an excellent cook, was hungry—as we all were—and he loudly lamented the fact that he wasn't in the middle of his own kitchen at home, where he could prepare a dinner instead of perishing of starvation in the middle of the desert.

In preparing this book, I recalled Van telling me about some of his great dishes and asked him for a menu.

❧❧ "Poor Man's" Beef Wellington ❧❧

3 eggs
2 pounds ground round steak
2 slices bread
½ cup cold water
1 teaspoon salt
1 teaspoon black pepper
2 tablespoons catsup
2 tablespoons Lea & Perrin's sauce
1 tablespoon prepared horseradish
1 tablespoon finely chopped ham
1 small onion (minced)
1 tablespoon prepared mustard
1 jigger brandy
1 unsliced liver sausage
1 package pie crust mix

Beat 2 eggs lightly and mix with meat. Break up bread and soak in water. Put into meat. Add everything else to meat with exception of liver sausage and pie crust mix. Knead with hands until mass forms a rather soft ball.

If using liver sausage with skin, remove skin. (Jones's liver sausage comes without skin.) Place sausage in middle of meat and mold meat around it into a round, square or oblong mass. Put in skillet with about ¼ inch of water. Bake in 350° (moderate) oven for 1½ hours. Look at it from time to time to see that the water hasn't evaporated. If it has, add more.

Remove meat from pan and let cool completely. Prepare pie crust mix according to directions on package and wrap around meat. Seal edges by brushing with egg. Put back into oven and cook according to pie crust package directions or until crust has turned a golden brown.

❧§❧ Au Gratin Potatoes ❧§❧

4 medium boiled potatoes   Breadcrumbs
Salt, pepper (to taste)   Butter or margarine
1 teaspoon flour   Milk
¼ pound sharp grated cheese

Slice potatoes about ⅛ inch thick. Place half of potatoes in greased casserole dish. Salt and pepper lightly. Sprinkle small amount of flour over all. Sprinkle cheese to cover. Dot with butter or margarine. Repeat same process with rest of potatoes. Pour milk to cover ⅔ of ingredients. Place layer of bread crumbs over all for better browning on top.

Place in preheated 350° oven and bake until potatoes are done (about 25 minutes).

❧§❧ Cauliflower with Lemon Parsley ❧§❧ Butter

Cauliflower   Lemon juice
Butter   Salt, pepper
1 teaspoon parsley (chopped)

Place cauliflower in salted boiling water and cook until tender (this will take about 10 minutes, but it is best to test with a fork). Drain. Top with melted butter to which has been added a teaspoon of chopped parsley and lemon juice to taste. Add pepper and salt.

❧§❧ Coffee Marshmallow Whip ❧§❧

1 pound marshmallows   Pinch salt
  (cut up)   1 pint whipping cream
1 cup strong coffee

Dissolve marshmallows in hot coffee in top of double boiler. Add salt. Let cool slightly and fold into stiffly beaten whipped cream. Refrigerate for at least three hours.

Striped Bass Aegean
Aegean Salad
Peaches Aegean
Coffee

Long before he knew Jackie Kennedy, I was aboard Aristotle Onassis's yacht, the *Christina,* for cocktails.

The elegance and grandeur of this ship with its El Grecos and other famous paintings, the solid gold fixtures, the private plane moored to the deck, have been described many times. What especially intrigued me was the bar with its clear glass top through which you could see a map of the sea with tiny little ships dotted across it. Noticing my interest, "Ari" pressed a button, whereupon all the ships began to sail. It was completely charming and, I believe, done with electromagnets. I was so fascinated by what I was seeing, I can only recall being served a whisky sour.

Ari is particularly fond of Greek food and often goes to fine Greek restaurants when he is away from home. One of his favorite places for lunch in New York is the Sea Fare of The Aegean, and this menu includes the dishes he orders frequently. The Peaches Aegean is a favorite dessert of Jackie O's. This is an original recipe with the restaurant.

Peaches Aegean come from Georgia, U.S.A., where all the Georgia peaches come from.

◆§§◆ Striped Bass Aegean ◆§§◆

5 pound striped bass (whole)	4 ounces dry sherry
2 tablespoons olive oil	2 tablespoons fresh lemon juice
2 tablespoons garlic butter	Dash of oregano
Salt, pepper (to taste)	¼ cup tomato juice
8 littleneck clams	¼ cup clam juice

Place fish in medium-size shallow pan. Bake it in olive oil and garlic butter, with salt and pepper, in preheated 400° oven for 20 minutes. Add remaining ingredients and place back in oven for 25 minutes or until done.

◆§§◆ Aegean Salad ◆§§◆

1 head romaine lettuce	4″ × 4″ piece Greek Feta
2 tomatoes	cheese
6 or 8 Spanish anchovies	Pinch oregano
1 head Boston iceberg lettuce	Salt, pepper (to taste)
1 lemon	2 or 3 black olives with pits
Olive oil	Italian parsley

Chop romaine lettuce. Cut tomatoes into 1-inch pieces. Chop anchovies into ¼-inch pieces. Cut Boston lettuce into small 1-inch portions but do not chop (pull apart with hands). Squeeze juice of lemon and add to olive oil to taste. Slice cheese into ¼-inch pieces. Crumble pinch of oregano in your hand and sprinkle over mixture. Add salt and pepper and black olives with pits (must include pits to give very full taste). Add a little chopped Italian parsley and mix all together thoroughly.

◆§§◆ Peaches Aegean ◆§§◆

1 tablespoon sugar
Metaxa brandy (about 1 jigger)
Stewed fresh peaches

Cook sugar over slow fire to point where it is ready to burn. Add brandy and mix with peach juice. Pour over peaches.

The amount of brandy or peach juice may vary depending on personal taste.

Eggplant Sophia Loren
Italian White Wine
Fresh Fruit with Italian Cheeses
Espresso

One year, the first question everyone asked when I returned from Italy was, "What is Sophia Loren *really* like? What did you two talk about?" I'm sure everyone expected me to tell them the latest international gossip that hadn't reached the papers.

I thought back to sitting with one of the most glamorous women in the world in one of the most magnificent villas decorated in breathtaking 17th-century decor—what did we talk about?

I didn't have a word of gossip to relate—it was pure and simply "girl talk." Much about Carlo Jr., of course. Then, "where did you buy it?"

The "where did you buy it" concerned a beautiful leather bag I was carrying. Sophia asked me to get her one just like it when I returned to the United States and charge it to her (which I did). It turned out that when she received the bag and examined it more closely, she found that it was made in Italy—by a manufacturer who was a close personal friend. She could have bought it wholesale or gotten one as a gift.

This recipe is one she loves. She learned it from her mother when she was a little girl living in Naples.

Sophia particularly loves Neapolitan dishes, and she eats pasta fearlessly. Forgetting whatever qualm I might have had about all that fattening food, I indulged along with her. But remembering an old line from Norma Shearer, I did say, "A moment on the lips, a lifetime on the hips." Sophia merely shrugged in typical Italian fashion. I couldn't help but wonder why it was so much more attractive and sexy on her hips than on mine! I gave an Italian shrug too—and went on a diet the next day.

I chose this eggplant recipe for the book rather than a pasta because it was a favorite dish and there already are so many pasta recipes. I hope you like my choice.

⋅🙞 *Eggplant Sophia Loren* 🙜⋅

2 medium eggplants
Olive oil
1 1-pound can Italian
  tomatoes
1 clove garlic

½ pound grated Parmesan
  cheese
1 medium Mozzarella cheese
1 pound salami (sliced)

Peel eggplants and slice about a ¼ inch thick. Cover with lightly salted water and soak for ½ hour. Dry, then sauté in oil to light golden color. In another pan cook tomatoes and garlic in 1 tablespoon oil on slow heat to sauce consistency.

In oiled baking pan put layer of eggplant, tomato sauce, Parmesan cheese, slices of Mozzarella, and salami. Repeat layers of same ingredients until pan is full, ending with a sprinkling of Parmesan cheese. Bake in a preheated 350° oven for 15 minutes. Serve hot or cold. This will serve 6.

Pearlie Mae's Baked Chicken with Onions
Zucchini with Corn
Rice Puddin'
Coffee

"I like to cook big," Pearl Bailey says. "When I'm cleanin' my house, and I really clean my house—some women talk about cleanin' their house but don't—I cook at the same time. Like yesterday, while I was cleanin' my house I was cookin' three different meats, plus bakin' a chicken, navy beans, zucchini with corn, makin' potato salad and rice puddin'. But I don't cook by any menu or recipe. I got to do it right out of my head.

"The funny part was when I was cookin' yesterday, I wasn't even hungry, but I like to have something ready if somebody comes in. There's nothin' worse than a man comin' home from a hard day's work and his wife sayin', 'What would you like to eat?' and she puts somethin' in the pressure cooker which only destroys food to me. This way I always got three or four choices in the refrigerator."

And having cooked since she was a very little girl, Pearlie Mae considers herself unexcelled at several dishes—she particularly favors her "Rice Puddin'."

"Be sure you wash the rice before," she cautions, then "no salt, no double boiler, no nutmeg or cinnamon. Just plenty of butter, eggs, milk, sugar, raisins, and lots of vanilla."

Since she doesn't use recipes, she has her own "tasting" system.

"I taste but I always wash the spoon," she says. She considers her judgment in seasoning to be unerring, due to her tasting system.

"You never have to put salt and pepper on *my* table," she says.

We finally pinned Pearl down a little more precisely, and as near as we can figure out, this is how she prepared a little after-theater snack she recently served to the cast.

☙ *Pearlie Mae's Baked Chicken* ☙
with Onions

Salt, pepper
2 4- to 6-pound roasting
chickens

Flour
6 large onions (sliced)

Salt and pepper chickens. Sprinkle lightly with flour. Place a bed of onions in roasting pan and pour from 4 to 6 cups of water over them. Add chickens, cover and let cook 3 to 3½ hours or until done. It will leave a very moist juice, gravy for some dry rice or mashed potatoes.

Editor's note: When this chicken is completed it will look just as white as when you put it in. Pearl Bailey likes it that way, but concedes that for some people, who prefer it toast color, you would have to remove the lid the last half hour to brown it.

☙ *Zucchini with Corn* ☙

Pearl's ecstatic about this zucchini mixture she discovered.

2 zucchinis
1 can tomatoes
1 large onion

1 clove garlic (chopped)
2 or 3 cups water
1 or 2 cans corn

Cut up zucchinis, tomatoes, onion, and garlic. Place in casserole dish and add water and corn. Cover and let simmer in 350° oven for 40 minutes.

❧ Rice Puddin' ❧

2 cups rice (*be sure to wash it*)
4 eggs
¼ cup sugar
½ pound butter

About 1 quart milk
1½ tablespoons vanilla
About 2 cups yellow raisins
Ice cream

Cook rice according to directions on box but do not put salt in water. Beat eggs. Add sugar, butter, and milk and mix thoroughly with beaten eggs. Stir in vanilla. Plump up raisins in a little water. Drain and add to mixture. Put in very well-greased casserole dish and bake in 325° oven for about 20 minutes.

Pearl adds this note of caution: "You've got to taste it before."

Editor's second note: We tested this three times and each time came out with definitely unsoft rice. In addition, a custard formed on the top. Returning to Pearl again, we learned that she doesn't like soft rice in her puddin' and it does always form a custard on top. When she serves it, she always puts a gob of ice cream on it.

Pork Chops
Spoon Bread
Fried Sauerkraut
Apollo 10's Chocolate "Scrub Cake"

At precisely 12:45 P.M. EDT, Sunday, May 18, 1969, Saturn-Apollo 10 rose deliberately, majestically, from its pad, with its crew of Colonel Thomas P. Stafford, Commander John W. Young, and Commander Eugene A. Cernan. A half second late in takeoff, the "delay" occasioned some tongue-in-cheek comments from media observers.

Talking with Kaye Stafford later, at a celebration party at Toots Shor's, I asked if she had to take tranquilizers before flights to quiet her nerves.

"Not at all," she replied. "I quiet whatever qualms I might have by baking a chocolate cake for Tom and bringing some of it to friends during the flight. I got the recipe several years ago in Oklahoma, but I've renamed it 'Scrub Cake' because after eating it, Tom always has to scrub the Mission twice before making it."

While men are in outer space exploring new planets, the wives are still very much "in space" in their kitchens.

I asked Kaye if I could have the recipe for one of our menus.

Within twenty-four hours Kaye had written the recipe precisely and mailed it. The wives of "our Astronauts" are wonderfully responsible women.

❧§❧ Pork Chops ❧§❧

4 thick pork chops
1 tablespoon butter
Black pepper
Paprika

1 tablespoon flour
Milk
½ cup strong coffee

Dust pork chops lightly with pepper and paprika. Brown in butter on both sides. Cover and reduce heat to low. Let cook 10 minutes on each side. Remove chops and retain just enough grease to cover bottom of pan. Reserve remaining grease to fry sauerkraut. Stir in flour. Add milk gradually and stir until gravy thickens. Add coffee and stir. Place chops in gravy. Cover and let simmer over low heat for about 10 minutes on each side.

❧§❧ Spoon Bread ❧§❧

2 cups boiling water
1 tablespoon butter
1½ teaspoons salt
1 cup yellow corn meal
4 eggs (separated)

½ cup milk
½ cup flour
2 tablespoons sugar
2 tablespoons baking powder

Have water hot in bottom of double boiler. Place two cups of boiling water in top of boiler. Add the butter, salt, and corn meal and stir until very thick. Remove from flame and transfer into bowl to cool. Meanwhile, beat 4 egg yolks into the milk and beat that into the mixture. Add flour and sugar and baking powder. Mix together thoroughly. Beat the 4 egg whites until very stiff and fold them in. Bake in a preheated oven at 425° for 50 to 55 minutes. Be sure that your casserole dish is well buttered and that you only fill it half full, as it will rise.

❧§❧ Fried Sauerkraut ❧§❧

Drain one can sauerkraut and pat with towel to get out excess moisture. Fry in pork chop drippings until lightly brown.

Apollo's 10's Chocolate "Scrub Cake"

2 cups sugar

2 cups flour

½ cup shortening

¼ pound butter

1 cup water

4 tablespoons cocoa

½ cup buttermilk

2 eggs (beaten)

1 teaspoon soda

1 teaspoon vanilla

Sift together the sugar and flour. In a saucepan bring to boil the shortening, butter, water, and cocoa. Pour over sugar and flour while still hot. Add the buttermilk, beaten eggs, soda, and vanilla. Bake in two 8″ × 8″ buttered pans in 400° oven for about 20 minutes. Test for doneness by inserting toothpick into cake. If it comes out clean, the cake is done. Remove from oven and place pan on cake rack and let cool for 10 to 15 minutes before removing it from pan. Then frost.

"SCRUB CAKE" FROSTING

6 tablespoons milk

¼ pound butter

4 tablespoons cocoa

1 pound powdered sugar

1 teaspoon vanilla

1 cup chopped nuts

Bring the milk, butter, and cocoa to a boil. Add the powdered sugar, vanilla, and nuts. Spread over cake while still hot.

Fish 'n' Chips à la Cary Grant

Our friendship with Cary Grant goes back twenty years. As a fan of his I'll never forget the first time we had dinner together at Romanoff's in Los Angels. Anxious to eat what he ate, I ordered everything he ordered—oysters, Maine lobster, etc.—only to be told by the maitre d' that they only had one order of each. Charming and attractive Cary gallantly told me he didn't care at all— his favorite dish was actually fish 'n' chips, served the way thousands of English pubs serve it, and if he couldn't have that he didn't care much what he ate.

Recently he told us that he had discovered a restaurant in Atlanta, Georgia, that rivaled the finest fish 'n' chips he ever ate in London, and that was Piper's Fish 'n' Chips at 215 Pharr Road.

This is such a delightful dish for patio or yard parties, or even coktail parties, that I thought you would like to have it English style.

Fish

1 egg	4 filets of bass, flounder, or
1 tablespoon vinegar	sole
1 tablespoon cold water	Bread or cracker crumbs

Beat egg with vinegar and water. Dip each filet into this and then roll in crumbs. Fry in 1½ inch hot fat in skillet until nicely browned on all sides. Drain on paper towel.

❦ *Chips* ❦

Actually the English chips are our French fries. It is simple to use the frozen French fries, but if you wish to make your own, wash and pare four medium-size potatoes and cut lengthwise in strips about ½ inch thick. Soak in cold water, then dry between towels. Fry in skillet of hot fat until potatoes are golden and tender. Drain on paper towel. Salt.

The English then make a bag of waxed paper and alternate bits of fish and potato. This is then wrapped in newspaper and you simply dip in and take whatever comes first. At a party there are usually plenty of salt and pepper shakers handy and lots of paper napkins.

The English are apt to eat this walking along the streets.

Carol Channing's Honey Scotch
Hello Dolly Cookies
Grandmother's Popcorn Balls

Carol Channing became a health food addict many years ago while visiting the Alfred Lunts on their farm. Carol had been plagued by throat trouble, and the Lunts advised her to eat only foods organically cultivated and her throat trouble would disappear. She would feel better, look better, and have more energy.

Carol followed their advice. Now, when traveling, she brings her own food and her own cook. If the hotel hasn't kitchen facilities, it installs a stove and refrigerator for her use. A typical day's menu might include for breakfast: El Molino buckwheat cakes and buckwheat honey, blueberries from Forstner Farms, blueberry tea. For dinner: Czimer goat, Puerto Rican taro roots, raw tomatoes from Barry Farms, Honey Scotch candy, and Rose Hip tea.

One evening, when we were dining with Carol and her husband, Charles Lowe, at the swank Colony restaurant in New York, they arrived carrying a large tote bag filled with thermos bottles. While all of us were ordering dinner, Carol merely ordered a hot plate for her meat and a cold plate for her salad, plus a cup. That night her meat consisted of six fried pork chops plus several little fried pork sausages. (It makes no difference how the food is cooked.) Over this she poured pork juice. Her salad consisted of several slices of cucumber that had been marinated. She explained that this was her "pork day with cucumbers." She eats no bread or dessert, but for her sweet tooth she carries with her Honey Scotch candy.

We have selected for Carol's recipes the items that would be easy to make from local stores.

Another famous star on a diet of organically cultivated and raised food is Gloria Swanson. She, however, does not bring her own food to a restaurant. When in a restaurant, she will first inquire as to whether they have such food, and if they do not she will give them a lecture on why they should. She will then order an avocado filled with fresh caviar—which would be acceptable on her diet, both being natural foods. Touring Italy one time and not being able to procure avocado and caviar, she subsisted on nuts.

Certainly we cannot argue the great vitality, energy, and beauty of these stars. While they might be able to promise you these qualities, unfortunately we can't promise you their talent as well.

✲✲✲ *Carol Channing's Honey Scotch* ✲✲✲

½ *cup water*   ½ *cup honey*
2 *cups sugar*

Heat water and sugar, stirring until sugar is dissolved. Add honey and cook, stirring gently just enough to prevent scorching. Cook to the hard-crack stage (300°). Remove from heat and pour candy into a buttered pan. When candy begins to set, cut into strips 1-inch wide. Roll into cylinders. Cut with a scissors into pieces 1-inch long. Yields 1 pound.

This recipe that Miss Channing uses is taken from *Very Basically Yours,* an allergy cookbook edited by the Board of the Human Ecology Study Group.

✲✲✲ *Hello Dolly Cookies* ✲✲✲

This recipe was presented to Carol when she played Little Rock, Arkansas, in *Hello, Dolly.* The Little Rock Cooking Club made up a basket of Hello Dolly Cookies for Miss Channing and also gave her permission to use their recipe.

Melt 1 stick of oleo in a 9″ × 12″ pan.

Pour 1 cup graham cracker crumbs over this and spread.

Pour 1 cup cocoanut over and spread.

Pour 1 package of chocolate chips over and spread (Carol uses 2 packages).

Pour 1 cup of nuts over this and spread.

Pour 1 can of Eagle Brand condensed milk over all.

Bake 30 minutes at 350°. Let cool completely before cutting.

❧ Grandmother's Popcorn Balls ❧

Carol believes that Christmas time means Popcorn Balls and candy. This German Popcorn Ball recipe was Carol's grandmother's special favorite.

1 cup sugar	*1 teaspoon vanilla*
½ cup corn syrup	*¼ teaspoon salt*
⅛ pound butter	*8 cups popped popcorn*

Mix together sugar, corn syrup, and butter. Stir over low flame until mixture comes to a boil. Cover for a few minutes. Remove the lid and place a candy thermometer into liquid. Cook without stirring to 270°. Remove from heat. Add the vanilla and salt. Test liquid by dropping a teaspoonful into cold water until mixture forms a soft ball. Pour over 8 cups of freshly popped corn which has been kept hot in the oven. Mix rapidly, making certain that all kernels are coated. If you like, the syrup may be colored with food coloring when you add the vanilla and salt. To make the popcorn balls, wet hands with cold water and take small quantity of mixture and press quickly into balls. Place on wax paper to cool.

Paprika Schnitzel à la Pasternak
Parsley Potatoes
Raw Spinach Salad with Bacon
Almond Cookies
Coffee

One of our dear, close friends is Joe Pasternak, the Hungarian-born motion picture producer who, if he weren't a producer, could have been a great chef. He may have introduced the joke, "To be a good Hungarian cook, first steal two eggs——"

Anxious to write a cookbook based on old family recipes, plus many Hungarian friends' secret recipes, Joe approached a publisher about printing such a book. He found the publisher skeptical about a wealthy, important producer knowing anything about cooking.

We invited Joe to use our kitchen as a testing laboratory for a dinner party that would include the publisher and a few friends.

We were in the living room enjoying cocktails. Joe, in an apron and tall chef's hat, was cooking and singing in the kitchen. Peeking out of the kitchen, Joe hailed the bartender and told him to bring him a very dry martini. The bartender drew me to one side and whispered, "Mrs. Wilson, the cook has asked for a drink. Is it all right to serve it to him?"

"By all means, as much as he wants," I replied. "You see he also happens to be the guest of honor."

These are some of the things Joe whipped up for us that night.

❧ *Paprika Schnitzel à la Pasternak* ❧

About 2 to 3 pounds veal
  steak (trimmed and sliced
  ½ inch thick)
1 teaspoon salt
¼ teaspoon pepper
1 tablespoon lemon juice
1 large onion
1 clove garlic
2 large bellpeppers
1 large steak tomato

Cooking oil, butter, or
  margarine
1 tablespoon pimento
1 tablespoon red paplika
1 cup chicken broth
2 tablespoons Marsala wine
Few dashes hot paprika,
  cayenne
Water if needed (optional)

Slice veal steaks ½ inch thick, trim, wash and dry them thoroughly with paper towels, and pound on both sides with a wooden mallet. Sprinkle meat lightly with a few dashes salt and pepper and a few drops lemon juice. Place in the refrigerator.

Meantime, mince onion and garlic. Peel and mince 1 bellpepper. Peel tomato, squeeze out all seeds and juices and dice. Heat cooking oil, butter, or margarine and sauté the vegetables until limp. Add pimento. Remove skillet from flame, sprinkle vegetables with paprika.

Remove meat from refrigerator and in separate pan fry both sides of the meat in cooking oil, butter or margarine, about 2 minutes each side.

Pour the chicken broth and Marsala wine over the vegetables. Bring to a boil and spoon over the meat. Cover the skillet and cook meat fork tender. Taste for seasoning. Add more water if needed for gravy.

Decorate with fresh bellpepper rings. Serves about 6.

❧ *Parsley Potatoes* ❧

2 pounds tiny new potatoes
1 teaspoon salt
½ teaspoon caraway seeds

2 tablespoons butter
1 tablespoon minced fresh
  parsley

Peel or scrape potatoes, wash and put them in a pot, cover with water. Add salt and caraway seeds to water. Boil until tender. Strain.

Heat butter and add to it parsley. Stir potatoes around in butter and parsley but do not break them. Serve separately or place around meat.

Raw Spinach Salad with Bacon

1 pound raw young spinach	1 teaspoon sugar
6 slices bacon	1/4 teaspoon salt
4 tablespoons red wine vinegar	1/4 teaspoon pepper

Wash spinach thoroughly. Trim off stalks and break or cut leaves into generous bite-size pieces. Place in bowl of cold water and crisp in refrigerator.

Fry bacon until crisp and drain. Mix vinegar in with bacon fat and add sugar, salt, and pepper. Pour dressing over spinach and crumble bacon on top. This dressing may be served two ways, either slightly cool over the crisp spinach or poured hot over the spinach (which will wilt spinach).

Almond Cookies

10 ounces grated almonds	2 egg whites
5 tablespoons sugar	Lemon icing

Cream the almonds, sugar, and egg whites together and knead well on a floured board. Roll 1/4 inch thick and cut little sticks from the dough. Bake in a 300° oven for about 5 minutes, or until set. Remove from the oven and cool, then frost with lemon icing.

LEMON ICING

2 1/2 cups powdered sugar	Juice of 1/2 lemon
2 egg whites	Grated rind of 1 lemon

Mix all the ingredients together and use as icing on cookies.

Caesar Salad
Diahann Carroll's Baked Potatoes with Caviar
Frosted Grapes
Espresso

Contrary to the lives of many artists who had a great deal of struggling to do before achieving success, Diahann Carroll's rise was meteoric from the beginning.

Born in the Bronx, New York, daughter of a subway conductor, her early life was reasonably comfortable. She wanted to be a singer, and attended the High School of Music and Art, graduated, and went on to New York University, where she decided to be a social worker dealing with psychiatric cases—but not for long.

Showman Lou Walters auditioned her for a revue. Nothing came of the revue, but Walters was so impressed with her singing talent that he got her a spot on the TV show *Chance of a Lifetime*, where she became the first girl to win three weeks in a row. A singing engagement at the Latin Quarter in New York immediately followed, then the Broadway stage, moving pictures, recordings, and her own television show.

Dedicated to her work and her daughter, Suzanne Ottillie, Diahann is equally at home in the kitchen as she is on the stage. A gourmet cook, she loves to plan and prepare mouth-watering menus and dishes.

One of her favorite menus for an after-theater supper is this easy and delicious one. Inexpensive too, compared to famous restaurants that serve these potatoes. For instance, El Morocco serves them for—are you ready?—$12 an order. However they *do* use fresh caviar. Diahann will show you how to get the same effect and taste for a dinner for two for only $3.

Try serving it with wine and candlelight, as they do at El Morocco.

❧ *Caesar Salad* ❧

1 head lettuce
1 romaine lettuce
Salt
Freshly ground pepper
2 tablespoons garlic butter
1 cup fried croutons
¾ cup olive oil
Garlic

1 tablespoon vinegar
½ tablespoon lemon juice
1 tablespoon Worcestershire
* sauce*
6 anchovies (cut in small
* pieces)*
Grated Parmesan cheese
1 coddled egg

Place crisped greens in salad bowl and sprinkle with salt and pepper. Fry croutons in garlic butter. Cool. Pour olive oil, vinegar, lemon, and Worcestershire sauce on salad and toss. Add anchovies. Sprinkle liberally with cheese. Add coddled egg. Toss and blend all together.

❧ *Diahann Carroll's Baked Potatoes* ❧ *with Caviar*

2 large baking potatoes
2 large pats butter
Salt

½ pint sour cream
1 2-ounce tin Romanoff caviar
* (Blue Label; about $2.50)*

Scrub potatoes and put in preheated 450° oven. (If you rub a little salad oil on the skins they'll come out crisper.) Bake for about 1 hour or until tender when pricked with a fork. Baked potatoes should never be sliced through with a knife. Prick through the center and then push from both ends so potato rises in center. This lets the steam escape and makes a fluffier potato. Place a pat of butter in the center and mash through. Salt very lightly. Place a heaping tablespoon of sour cream on top, and an ounce of caviar on top of this.

❧ Frosted Grapes ❧

Seedless grapes
1 egg white

1 tablespoon finely granulated sugar
1 tablespoon powdered sugar

Dip clusters of grapes in slightly beaten egg white. When nearly dry, swirl around in granulated sugar and then in powdered sugar. Wave cluster around in the air a few times and then lay on rack to completely dry.

Raquel Welch Filet of Sole with Lobster Sauce
Asparagus Vinaigrette
Lemon Ice Topped with Crème de Menthe
Coffee

On a trip to Vietnam with Bob Hope's USO troupe, Raquel Welch and all the rest laughed when the first meal was served aboard the big transport plane, then nosing out over the Pacific. The meal was not served by lovely stewardesses from a neat airline kitchen. It was served by GIs, and it was Chicken Delight. There were also soft drinks, cans of beer, and even a bar for the thirsty.

Beautiful Raquel, one of the world's favorite pinup girls, was to have more experience with chicken later. At every base in Vietnam that the troupe visited, the GI cooks had prepared fried chicken, and Raquel, like the rest of the performers, rushed around backstage at the temporary theaters nibbling at a chicken leg.

Raquel has lived in Italy, England, and of course in America, and she has her own tastes.

"I always found that you can tell how distinctive a restaurant is by how well it cooks nondistinctive dishes," she told us. "Every restaurant has remarkable specialties of the house. Humphrey Bogart, after winning his Oscar, said you could only really judge a best performance by an actor if you lined up all the actors and let each do *Hamlet*. Well, Eggs Benedict and Steak Diane are like *Hamlet*—all the really fine restaurants have them on their menus, but the Dorchester in London wins the Oscar."

Since earlier recipes were given for Eggs Benedict and Steak Diane, we present another one of Raquel Welch's favorites.

⋙ Filet of Sole with Lobster Sauce ⋙

Poach 4 filets in ½ water and ½ white wine. Fish is done when easily flaked with a fork (about 2 to 3 minutes). Drain. Place on hot platter and cover with lobster sauce.

LOBSTER SAUCE

3 tablespoons butter	2 egg yolks
Salt, pepper, paprika (to taste)	1 cup lobster meat
Cream	2 tablespoons sherry

Heat butter in skillet over low flame. Add seasonings. Slowly stir in cream and simmer to reduce slightly, stirring often. Beat yolks in a bowl. Remove skillet from flame and beat yolks a little at a time into cream and butter. Add lobster and return to fire. Stir constantly until sauce thickens (do not let sauce come to a boil). Add sherry and check seasonings.

⋙ Asparagus Vinaigrette ⋙

½ cup olive oil	1 tablespoon pimento
4 tablespoons tarragon vinegar	(chopped)
3 tablespoons sweet pickle relish	½ teaspoon salt
2 tablespoons chopped parsley	½ teaspoon pepper
1 hard-boiled egg (riced)	½ teaspoon sugar
1 teaspoon chopped chives	Cooked or canned asparagus (green or white)

Blend oil with vinegar. Season and add remaining ingredients. Chill before serving over asparagus.

⋙ Lemon Ice Topped with ⋙ Crème de Menthe

Place scoop of lemon ice in dish. Make small indentation and fill with crème de menthe.

"Arf" Hamburger
Baked Bananas
Cole Slaw with Gingered Sour Cream
Rosé Wine

It was a swelteringly hot summer day in New York when Paula Prentiss and her husband, Richard Benjamin, invited Earl for lunch and an interview at the Stage 73, an Off-Broadway theater. The idea intrigued Earl, for Dick was directing Paula in *Arf* and her role was that of a dog named Fido.

Having learned that Paula was going to prepare the lunch, Earl picked up a bottle of rosé wine along the way. They were as delighted as if he had brought them rare champagne, saying no interviewer had ever come bringing liquor.

Earl was questioning Paula about how she could possibly portray the role of a dog convincingly. Being a very talented young girl, Paula set out to show him. Down to the floor she went on her hands and knees, jumping around, wagging her head and barking "Arf!" Earl was still amazed, when she hopped onto his lap and began licking his face! Now Paula isn't just talented, she's a very attractive girl as well, and after a few seconds he thought it the better part of valor to say, "Good doggie—*down!*"

I thought you'd like to know what Paula not only eats—but cooks.

❧ "Arf" Hamburger ❧

2 pounds freshly ground
   hamburger
½ cup celery (finely
   chopped)
1 tablespoon Worcestershire
   sauce
Salt, pepper (to taste)

4 tablespoons chutney
   (drained and chopped)
½ pound fresh sharp Cheddar
   cheese
1 tomato (sliced)
2 English muffins (split)

Combine hamburger with celery, Worcestershire sauce, salt, and pepper. Place 1 tablespoon chutney in middle of hamburger and mold around it. Do *not* mix into the hamburger. Brown patties in a little butter in pan. Remove and place on half a toasted English muffin. Place a slice of tomato on top and then a slice of cheese. Broil long enough to melt cheese.

❧ Baked Bananas ❧

Bananas
Sugar
Cinnamon

Butter
Sherry

Cut unpeeled bananas lengthwise. Sprinkle with sugar mixed with cinnamon and dot with butter. Place under broiler or grill long enough to melt butter and sugar, and until bananas are warmed through. Pour ½ teaspoon sherry on top of each.

❧ Cole Slaw with Gingered Sour Cream ❧

1 head cabbage
3 tablespoons olive oil
1 tablespoon tarragon vinegar
¼ teaspoon salt

¼ teaspoon pepper
1 level teaspoon ginger
   powder
½ pint sour cream

Chop cabbage very fine and place in refrigerator to chill. Blend oil and vinegar with seasonings and mix into sour cream. Marinate slaw with dressing and serve.

The President and Mrs. Johnson

request the pleasure of the company of

Mr. and Mrs. Wilson

at dinner

on Wednesday evening, May 8, 1968

at eight o'clock

Black Tie

Dinner

Wente
Pinot
Chardonnay

Turban of Sole

Beaulieu
Cabernet
Sauvignon

Roast Sirloin of Beef
Dauphine Potatoes
Asparagus Hollandaise

Bibb Lettuce
Assorted Cheeses

Almaden
Blanc de Blancs

Vacherin Thankolsook

The White House
Wednesday, May 8, 1968

⋅ई॰॰

Turban of Sole
Roast Sirloin of Beef
Dauphine Potatoes
Asparagus Hollandaise
Bibb Lettuce
Assorted Cheeses
Vacherin Thankolsook

I never dreamed that one day I would be having dinner at the White House with the President of the United States. I was thrilled. I'm not one to keep souvenirs, but this invitation and menu I put away. Maybe some day a grandchild of mine will say to my son, "Gee, Dad, did she really?"

Everyone wanted to cluster around the President, and I was no exception. At the moment two Washington newspaper women had his ear and I couldn't get a word in edgewise. Then I heard the President say to them, "You girls have been old, old friends of mine for a long, long time." With that he leaned down from his great height and kissed them both on the cheek. And there I was still standing.

I thought, "Now or never," and tugged at his sleeve saying, "Mr. President, could an old, old girl be a new, new friend?"

And do you know, the President bent down and kissed me, too!

⋅ई॰॰ *Turban of Sole* *⋅ई॰॰*

4 filets of sole   *White wine*

A turban of sole is a filet wound around in a spiral effect just like a turban. Stick a toothpick in each one to hold them while you lay them in the pan. Simmer in wine to cover until sole easily flakes with a fork. Remove and drain.

SAUCE

1 tablespoon minced onion	½ cup cream
⅛ pound butter	About 3 ounces pâté de foie
4 mushrooms (chopped very	gras or liver pâté
fine)	Salt, pepper (to taste)
1 tablespoon flour	½ jigger sherry

Prepare sauce by sautéing onions in butter very delicately. Do not brown. Add mushrooms and sauté 1 or 2 minutes. Remove mushrooms from pan. Sprinkle pan with flour and slowly add cream. Stir constantly until cream has slightly thickened. Replace mushrooms and add pâté and seasonings. Stir all together and mix in sherry.

Fill tiers of fish with sauce. Spoon remaining sauce over all.

❧❧ Roast Sirloin of Beef ❧❧

Have meat at room temperature before roasting. Salt and pepper liberally. Preheat oven for about 10 minutes at 325°. Place meat, fat side up, in roaster. For rare, cook 18 to 20 minutes per pound; medium, 22 to 25 minutes; well done, about 30 minutes.

There are very little drippings from roast beef. Using whatever juices there are, add beef stock and thicken with a little flour and milk. Add a little Kitchen Bouquet or strong coffee for more flavor and coloring. Salt and pepper to taste.

❧❧ Dauphine Potatoes ❧❧

Mashed potatoes	Bread crumbs
Salt & pepper	Butter and cooking oil
1 egg (lightly beaten)	

Press seasoned mashed potatoes into small balls or oblong shapes. Dip in egg and bread crumbs and fry gently in half butter and half cooking oil until brown on all sides. They should be crusty on the outside and soft in the center.

❧❧❧ Asparagus Hollandaise ❧❧❧

With paring knife, remove scales from asparagus that hold sand and grit. With potato peeler, scrape bottom 2 inches of stalk. Wash and cook in boiling water to which has been added 1 teaspoon of salt. Boil uncovered for 5 minutes. Cover and cook until tender (about 10 to 15 minutes all together). Test with fork. Drain and add sauce.

HOLLANDAISE SAUCE

¼ *pound butter*	¼ *teaspoon salt*
4 egg yolks	*Dash cayenne pepper*
1 tablespoon lemon juice	

Melt butter in top of double boiler. (Have water hot but not at boiling stage. Water should never touch top of boiler.) Beat yolks to thick lemon color. Add to butter and stir constantly until mixture thickens. Add lemon juice, salt, and pepper.

If sauce should separate or begin to curdle, add a few drops of boiling water at the first sign.

❧❧❧ Bibb Lettuce ❧❧❧

Wash lettuce thoroughly and put in refrigerator to crisp.
The White House used a basic French dressing to which was added a little catsup.

❧❧❧ Assorted Cheeses ❧❧❧

This was a large platter of Brie, Camembert, and Gruyère.

❧❧❧ Vacherin Thankolsook ❧❧❧

I had never tasted Vacherin before (I believe the Thankolsook was added on in honor of one of the guests). Basically, it seemed quite simple except for one ingredient. Set before me was a meringue shell filled with raspberries and topped with whipped cream. However, when I tasted it I discovered on the meringue and under the berries was something that tasted like marzipan or almond paste. At first I was going to write to Mrs. Johnson, but then I felt a little foolish writing the wife of the President for a recipe as though she were the girl next door.

Finally I found a recipe for it in a fancy French cookbook, but it seemed quite involved so I experimented on my own. It looks and tastes the same.

MERINGUE SHELLS WITH ALMOND PASTE

3 egg whites
3/8 teaspoon salt
3/4 teaspoon cream of tartar
3/4 cup granulated sugar

1/4 teaspoon white vinegar
1/4 teaspoon vanilla
Almond paste

Preheat oven to 275°.

Have egg whites at room temperature (if you separate eggs and let stand in a bowl, they'll warm faster). Add salt and cream of tartar and beat until mixture forms rounding peaks. Beat in sugar a tablespoon at a time and continue beating until sugar has dissolved and mixture forms glossy pointed peaks (taste to be sure sugar has dissolved). This will take about 15 minutes with an electric beater. Add vinegar and vanilla and beat about 5 minutes more.

Drop by heaping tablespoons onto ungreased wrapping or other unglazed paper on a baking sheet. A pastry bag might help in forming shells, but I twirl a spoon in mixture until I have a hollow center. Bake for 30 minutes.

Meanwhile, make a medium stiff paste of 1 tablespoon almond paste and a little cream to soften. Remove shells and place paste in bottom and slightly up sides. This is very sweet so don't put in much—about 1/8 inch. Return meringues to the oven and let bake another 15 minutes or a little longer if you want them browner. At end of baking period, turn off oven and let stand in oven until cool.

Fill with berries and top with whipped cream.

The next time I tried this I put in the meringues almond-flavored macaroons that I had mashed with a rolling pin, and it turned out very well and was simpler.

P.S. Devotees of Vacherin will probably have my head for this recipe.

Chicken-Fried Steak
Boiled Potatoes
Boiled Onions
Romaine Lettuce with Garlic Dressing
Golden Pastries
Coffee

This is Earl's favorite dinner. He enjoys it so much that if there is any left over, I wrap it up and he will eat it late at night, cold. It is so simple and tasty, I thought you might like it, too.

Chicken-Fried Steak

2 pounds eye-round steak	4 tablespoons flour
(½ inch thick)	4 tablespoons butter
Salt, pepper (to taste)	4 tablespoons shortening

Sprinkle meat liberally with salt and pepper. Dredge both sides with the flour. Place Saran wrap around both meat and flour and pound with mallet or edge of saucer, for a few minutes. Remove wrap and place meat in melted butter and shortening in hot skillet. Fry steak until brown and crispy on both sides (about 15 minutes). Add leftover flour to pan and brown. Gradually pour in potato water, bring to boil, and stir vigorously to make gravy. Add more salt if desired.

❧ Boiled Potatoes ❧

Pare small new potatoes and cook in boiling unsalted water until tender. Drain. Add salt. Earl likes these with the gravy on top.

❧ Boiled Onions ❧

Peel outer layer off small onions and cook in boiling water until tender (about 25 to 35 minutes). Drain and transfer to dish. Pour over them browned butter to which a few drops of lemon juice has been added. Season with salt, pepper, and paprika to taste.

❧ Romaine Lettuce with Garlic Dressing ❧

2 medium-size cloves of garlic   4 tablespoons lemon juice
2 teaspoons salt   Romaine lettuce
8 tablespoons olive oil

Mash garlic and salt thoroughly together. Add olive oil and lemon juice. Stir. Mix with romaine until all leaves are coated.

❧ Golden Pastries ❧

½ pound butter   1 teaspoon vanilla
2 cups flour   ½ teaspoon cinnamon
6 egg yolks   1 cup ground nuts
4 egg whites   Powdered sugar
1 cup sugar

Work butter and flour like a pie pastry. Add egg yolks one at a time (unbeaten), mixing each one well into flour and butter. Form into ball and place in refrigerator until it becomes a hard mass of dough.

Beat egg whites stiff. Add sugar, vanilla, cinnamon, and nuts. Cut off pieces of the dough and roll out into thin sheets, cutting pieces about 3 inches square. Place a teaspoon of the egg-white mixture at one side of the squares of dough and fold over about 2 or 3 times. Bake on a slightly floured cookie sheet 20 minutes in a 350° oven until a delicate brown. Sprinkle with powdered sugar.

Tomato Gin Soup
Toots's Barbecued Spareribs
Brandied Tomatoes
Oranges in Crème de Menthe and Vodka

I ASKED MY HUSBAND TO WRITE THIS AS IT'S REALLY IN THE SALOON DEPARTMENT.

On Election Day in most states, the bars are closed until the polls close—obviously to prevent people from voting while under the influence of liquor. Because the day does have a holiday feeling in some places (with some offices being closed part of the day), there are people who insist on having some alcohol by getting it in their food. And so they have treasured recipes of the dishes that contain "spirits." They maintain it is quite possible to get intoxicated without having a drink.

The chief advocate of this policy is probably restaurateur Toots Shor who, during a 12 A.M. curfew in World War II, said, "Anybody who can't get drunk by midnight ain't tryin'!"

Toots is the authority for the remarkable statement, "Whisky never hurt anybody." He is passionately loyal to friends and his family. A friend asked his wife if it were true that she took him his breakfast each day.

"Yes," she said, "every morning I take Toots two bottles of Coke" (for hangovers).

But he discourages some drunks from overdoing it. "You're giving booze a bad name," he warns them.

One night his friends tried to get him to go home. They got him to the front door of his restaurant and into a cab. As the cab started away, Toots said to the driver, "Take me to Toots Shor's."

Some customers want to stay there almost as much as Toots does. One night one of them, a sportswriter, was being urged to get some sleep. A friend who'd brought him there for dinner said, "I want to drive you home." The sportswriter retorted, "You already have."

One of Toots's every-night drinking companions has been comedian Joe E. Lewis. "Don't mind Toots," Joe E. has said. "He's rude and loud—but he's also very annoying."

Toots is proud of being an old-timer. A young singer told a café audience, including Toots, "I'm going to sing some old songs for you—I hope you remember them." Toots yelled out, "Don't worry about us—just *you* remember them."

Here are some of Toots's suggestions for Election Day dining.

⋙ *Tomato Gin Soup* ⋙

2 cans tomato soup
1½ cans of water
Salt, pepper (to taste)
8 teaspoons whipped cream

4 teaspoons gin
2 teaspoons toasted almonds
(chopped)

Simmer tomato soup and water, season with a little salt and pepper. When hot, pour into cups. Add 2 teaspoons of stiffly whipped cream to each cup and 1 teaspoon of gin drizzled on the cream. Top with almonds. Makes 4 cups.

⋙ *Toots's Barbecued Spareribs* ⋙

4 pounds spareribs
1 cup vinegar
2½ tablespoons Worcester-
    shire sauce
Dash Tabasco sauce
1 tablespoon sugar
1 tablespoon olive oil

1 teaspoon dry mustard
½ cup catsup
½ teaspoon salt
½ teaspoon pepper
½ teaspoon paprika
1 jigger bourbon

Roast spareribs in shallow open pan in 450° oven for half an hour. Pour off fat.

Meanwhile, mix together all other ingredients to make sauce and simmer for 15 minutes. Cut spareribs in portions of 2 ribs each and place in broiler about 5 inches from low flame. Brush with sauce and turn frequently, every 10 minutes if possible, brushing each time. Cook until crisp (about 1 hour, depending on how meaty ribs are).

~§~ Brandied Tomatoes ~§~

⅓ cup olive oil	1 tablespoon dried dill
1 teaspoon salt	2 tablespoons brandy
1 tablespoon dried tarragon	2 beefsteak tomatoes

Combine all ingredients except tomatoes and let marinate for 10 minutes. Pour over thickly sliced tomatoes.

~§~ Oranges in Crème de Menthe ~§~ and Vodka

Marinate mandarin oranges in crème de menthe and vodka in refrigerator for about half an hour before serving. Top with toasted cocoanut.

Cassoulet l'Etoile
Artichoke and Watercress Salad
Burgundy Wine
Camembert Cheese with Toasted Crackers

They say, "The way to a man's heart is through his stomach."
So what about Elizabeth Taylor, who is Room Service's best friend?

Here is a celebrity who found that there are other routes to
a man's heart. She has not been seen in the kitchen getting all
perspirey lately. "She is not interested in cooking itself," states
a friend. "She is, however, interested in the results of cooking."

She loves hot dogs from Nathan's in New York, chili from
Chasen's in Hollywood, California, steaks from Gallagher's, New
York, lamb stew from Dinty Moore's in New York, and other
comparatively hearty dishes. And we once saw her do very well
at Teddy's, an Italian restaurant on West Broadway in downtown
New York. But she is also at home at Maxim's or La Tour D'Argent
in Paris.

On the Burton yacht, the *Kalizma*, there's no need for Elizabeth to cook, because the staff includes a chef and assistant. Nevertheless, the Burtons have been known to get hungry for French
dishes as they are made in America. One dish is Cassoulet—a so-
called French peasant dish—which is an extravagant version of
"pork and beans" with goose and sausages added. On two occasions
L'Etoile, the elegant French restaurant off 5th Avenue in New
York City, packaged Cassoulet in dry ice and air-shipped it to
the Burtons—who were in Paris at the time.

Richard Burton found the Cassoulet very good also at the Mont St. Michel restaurant on West 57th Street in New York City. In his days of *Hamlet* in New York, he was known to take Elizabeth there for a small feast after the theater.

❧ Cassoulet l'Etoile ❧

3 *pounds white beans*	2 *pounds breast of lamb*
1 *onion*	1 *clove garlic*
Cloves	1 *teaspoon flour*
2 *carrots*	6 *fresh tomatoes*
Salt, pepper	1 *gallon stock*
1 *garlic sausage*	*Bread crumbs*
1 *duckling*	*Chopped parsley*
12 *ounce salt pork*	½ *pound butter*
1 *pound shoulder of lamb*	

In addition to above ingredients you will need a *mirepoix* (mixture) of ½ cup carrots, ½ cup onions, ½ cup celery and one small clove garlic (all minced).

Soak the beans overnight; parboil them. Change the water and add onion stuck with cloves, carrots, salt, pepper, sausage and salt pork to beans. Cook until done.

Cut the duck and lamb into medium-sized pieces; season with salt and pepper. Saute in butter in a braising pan. When the meat begins to take color add the mirepoix. Let simmer. Drain fat, then mix in the flour. Place in oven for about five minutes. Add tomatoes and stock sufficient to cover. Finish cooking. When done, remove the meat and set aside. Use about one soup ladle of the cooking sauce to moisten the beans, which are being prepared separately.

In an earthenware casserole put lamb, duck, beans and sauce. Slice the sausage and salt pork and place on top in a decorative way. Sprinkle with bread crumbs mixed with parsley. Moisten with a little melted butter and place in oven to brown. Serve very hot. Will serve ten.

Artichoke and Watercress Salad

2 bunches watercress
1 tablespoon chopped parsley
1 tablespoon dill
1 tablespoon chili sauce
French dressing
4 artichoke bottoms

Cut stems off watercress right up to where leaves begin. Wash and pack in ice cubes in refrigerator to crisp.

Add parsley, dill, and chili sauce to French dressing and mix thoroughly.

Place artichoke in center of plate with watercress surrounding and slightly overlapping. Spoon over dressing.

Shrimp in Avocado
Garlic Bread
Fettucine al Burro
Veal Parmigiana
White Sangría
Barbra's Fool-Proof Chocolate Cake

When Barbra Streisand first heard the call of the wild to "go West young girl" and seek your fortune—she went.

She didn't go on horseback or by covered wagon to seek gold, however. She took a forty-minute subway ride from her home in Brooklyn to the show business world of Manhattan and struck pay dirt. And the further west she went, the more gold she struck. She became a stage star, a movie star, and a multimillion record seller; and her one-woman show in Central Park drew the largest crowd ever assembled to hear a single performer.

A "funny girl," Barbra: nonconforming, fiercely proud and even more determined. What she loves most about her meteoric career is that she did it without having her nose fixed, her teeth capped, or her name changed. Bravo! There are few that can achieve success on their own terms.

What she likes most of all about her menu is her "Fool-Proof" cake. It would be like Barbra to stir up something like that. With her enormous talent, everything she has done has been a cakewalk.

❧§❧ Shrimp in Avocado ❧§❧

2 ripe avocados
1 lemon
1 pound small shrimp
1 tablespoon vinegar
1 bay leaf

Salt, pepper
1 cup mayonnaise
2 tablespoons catsup
1 tablespoon sour cream

Cut each avocado lengthwise. Peel and pit each half. Rub a slice of lemon over the entire surface to prevent browning. Put in covered bowl and refrigerate.

Cook the shrimp in 1 quart water with 1 tablespoon vinegar, 1 bay leaf, and a dash of pepper. Shell and clean. Unless shrimp are very tiny, cut each in half.

Put mayonnaise, catsup, sour cream, salt and pepper, and juice of 1 lemon into a bowl and mix well. Add the shrimp. Put shrimp mixture inside the hollow of each avocado half. Serve on a bed of lettuce with a tomato slice on each plate.

❧§❧ Fettucine al Burro ❧§❧

2 cups broad noodles
½ cup butter

½ cup grated Parmesan cheese

Cook noodles according to package directions. Drain and put on a hot platter. Add butter. Toss until noodles are fully coated. Sprinkle with cheese and pass more cheese at table.

❧§❧ Veal Parmigiana ❧§❧

2 eggs
Salt, pepper (to taste)
1 cup seasoned bread crumbs
3 tablespoons grated Parmesan cheese
1 pound veal cutlets (cut from leg in slices)

3 tablespoons oil
3 tablespoons butter or margarine
1 can tomato paste
½ pound Mozzarella cheese

Beat eggs thoroughly and add salt and pepper. Mix bread crumbs with grated cheese. Dip cutlets in egg, then in bread crumbs. Fry in hot oil and butter about 3 minutes on each side or until golden. Place cutlets in baking pan with layer of tomato paste on top. Place thin slices of Mozzarella over tomato paste. Bake in 325° oven for 15 minutes or until cheese turns slightly brown.

❧ White Sangría ❧

This is best when made according to individual taste and according to which fresh fruits are in season. The kind of things to include are:

Chilled Italian or French white
    wine
Cut up oranges, lemons,
    peaches, apples or
    any other fruit

2 tablespoons sugar
1 jigger brandy
1 jigger Cointreau
1 tray ice cubes

Put all ingredients, including ice cubes, in a large pitcher. Stir and allow the ice to cool the drink.

❧ Barbra's Fool-Proof Chocolate Cake ❧

¼ pound butter
1¼ cup sugar
2 eggs
½ pint sour cream
2 teaspoons baking powder

1 teaspoon baking soda
1½ cups flour
⅓ cup Dutch cocoa
1 tablespoon cooled coffee
1 teaspoon vanilla

Cream butter and sugar and add whole eggs. Add sour cream alternately with dry ingredients, which have been sifted together three times. Add coffee and vanilla. Bake at 375° in two 9-inch layer tins for 20 minutes, then about 10 minutes more at 350°.

Frosting

9 *heaping tablespoons*
  confectioner's sugar

3 *heaping tablespoons*
  unsweetened Dutch cocoa
½ *pint sweet cream*

Sift together confectioner's sugar and Dutch cocoa. Add, stirring constantly, about ⅔ of a half pint of sweet cream (add a little at a time for good consistency). Frost cake.

For an extra special treat, serve the cake à la mode with coffee ice cream.

Beef and Kidney Pie à la Rex
Dumplings
Bean Salad with Vinegar Dressing
English Apple Pie
Tea

We were having cocktails with Rex Harrison in his suite at the Connaught Hotel in London. He apologized for his wife, Rachel, not being on hand to greet us, but explained that she had gone to a friend's to make his favorite dish, a beef and kidney pie, as it was his birthday. As soon as she put it in the oven and wiped the flour off her hands, she would be back.

A few moments later a breathless Rachel arrived and we sat around talking. Suddenly Rex asked, "Who's watching the pie?"

"Good heavens, I am," Rachel replied, whereupon we all grabbed our coats and ran.

The pie was a little brown on top but delicious.

Beaf and Kidney Pie à la Rex

⅓ cup flour
¼ teaspoon pepper
½ teaspoon celery salt
1½ pounds stewing beef
    (cut into 1-inch cubes)
½ cup butter or bacon fat
¼ cup minced onion

1 cup strong coffee
1 cup bouillon (cubes or
    canned)
1 cup red wine
½ teaspoon salt
½ teaspoon Worcestershire
    sauce

In bowl combine flour, pepper, and celery salt. Drop in meat, a few pieces at a time. Coat well. Reserve leftover flour. Heat fat in deep skillet; brown floured meat on all sides, a few pieces at a time (15 to 20 minutes). Remove pieces as they brown. When all meat has been browned, add the minced onion to the fat; simmer until just tender. Stir in reserved flour and blend.

Pour into large kettle and slowly stir in coffee, bouillon, wine, salt, and Worcestershire sauce. Cover and simmer over low flame about 2 hours, or until meat is tender.

Veal Kidneys

2 veal kidneys   ⅛ pound butter

Remove any outer membrane from kidneys. Slice in ¼ inch strips. With scissors remove fat and white veins. Wash and dry between towel.

Melt butter and sauté kidneys, turning frequently (about 5 to 6 minutes, or until just tender). Add kidneys to beef and transfer to casserole dish.

Pie Crust

Use packaged pie crust mix for crust (follow package directions). Cover top of casserole and prick with toothpick to let out steam. Bake until crust is light brown.

Dumplings

I usually make my dumplings from a Bisquick mix and find them delicious. If you wish to make your own, a friend gave me this recipe which is also very good.

2 cups flour   2 eggs (well beaten)
4 teaspoons baking powder   ⅔ cup milk
1 teaspoon salt   Diluted consommé
1 tablespoon vegetable oil

Sift flour, baking powder, and salt. Add vegetable oil, eggs, and milk a little at a time until you have a heavy batter. Drop with a teaspoon into boiling diluted consommé. Cover tightly and cook 10 to 12 minutes without removing the lid.

◆§◆ Bean Salad with Vinegar Dressing ◆§◆

2 10-ounce cans string beans
2 tablespoons minced onions
1 teaspoon salt
2 tablespoons olive oil
1 tablespoon sugar

½ cup wine vinegar
¼ teaspoon pepper
½ teaspoon dried tarragon
Paprika

Drain beans and cool. Combine remaining ingredients and toss lightly with beans. Chill for several hours. Dust with paprika.

◆§◆ English Apple Pie ◆§◆

Apples
½ cup white sugar
1 cup brown sugar

1 tablespoon flour
1 heaping tablespoon butter

Slice apples about ½ inch thick and place in buttered pie tin or Pyrex dish. Sprinkle ½ cup white sugar on top. Mix brown sugar with flour and sprinkle on top of this. Dot with butter. Bake in 325° oven for 30 minutes. May be served with sweetened whipped cream or hard sauce.

HARD SAUCE

2 ounces butter
4 ounces confectioners' sugar

1 tablespoon rum, brandy, or bourbon

Blend butter and sugar until creamy. Add liquor and mix well. Let set about 1 hour before using. Do not place in refrigerator.

From the Kitchen of...

So many good friends, upon learning of this cookbook, have helpfully sent in their best and most private recipes. We would like to conclude with a variety of suggestions from which you might enjoy making up your own menu.

Mrs. "Marty" Allen
BEVERLY HILLS

Boeuf Bourguignon à la "Marty"

"Frenchie," the attractive blond wife of the famous comedian, says this is her most successful buffet supper dish. However, "Marty" doesn't eat mushrooms, so she omits them.

Brown 3 pounds of lean boneless beef cut into 2-inch chunks in 1 tablespoon butter or cooking oil. Then add 2 tablespoons chopped shallots and brown those. Stir in 1 large tablespoon potato starch or 2 tablespoons flour and cook until slightly brown (be careful not to burn). Remove from flame and let cool a little. Pour in 1 cup beefstock, 1 pint water, 2 cups dry red wine, ½ cup any brandy, and 1 tablespoon tomato paste. Stir constantly. Put back on flame and stir until sauce thickens. Then add 1 teaspoon chopped garlic, 1 teaspoon dried thyme, 2 bouquet garni of parsley and 1 bay leaf tied together, freshly ground black pepper, 2 tablespoons chopped parsley, and 1 or 2 teaspoons salt.

Put into casserole and place in preheated 350° oven. Cook for 2 to 3 hours, stirring several times. For the last hour add 24 small white onions that have been skinned and browned in butter. At this time, add 1 pound mushrooms if desired. "If mushrooms are used you will need 3 extra tablespoons butter or cooking oil in skillet.) A half hour before finishing, add ⅓ cup of strawberry or raspberry marmalade.

This is better made the day before and reheated when ready to serve.

❦

Mrs. Marcel Aubry
New York

Aperitif Celery Delight

Germaine, wife of the French-born banker and financier, serves this tidbit with an aperitif or cocktail before dinner.

Wash and scrape celery and cut into bite-size pieces. Crisp in refrigerator. Just before serving, fill with steak tartare and sprinkle with capers.

❦

The Late Paula Ben Gurion
Israel

David's Breakfast

The late Paula Ben Gurion was concerned about her husband's weight and fed him only sugarless food in order to prevent his "putting on weight." She concocted this delicious and nourishing pap that he enjoyed. Their daughter was kind enough to give the recipe for this book.

Blend into pap 1 cup of yogurt, ¼ pound farmer's cheese, raspberry juice to taste, and half a can of apple juice.

❧❦❧

Mrs. J. Earle Brown
FORT WORTH

Glorified Pizza

"Joanie" to her friends, Mrs. Brown is equally well known as a charming hostess in both Fort Worth and Palm Springs, Calif.

Place on top of a frozen pizza a slice of sharp Cheddar cheese and slices of pimento olive. Bake according to pizza directions.

❧❦❧

Mrs. John Browning
OGDEN, UTAH

Hot Chutney Appetizer

Carol and her husband, the famous Browning Rifle Corporation head, enjoy this appetizer with their cocktails.

Cut white bread into squares or rounds. Toast one side. Spread untoasted side with peanut butter and 1 teaspoon chutney. Sprinkle with crumbled crisp bacon. Place in 350° oven until hot. Serve.

❧❦❧

Mrs. Martin Burden
NEW YORK

Shrimp and Mushroom Curry

Mrs. Burden's husband, the "Dining Out Tonight" columnist of the New York *Post,* brings us this recipe that she serves when they are not dining out.

The day before, mix ¾ cup all-purpose flour, 7 or 8 teaspoons curry powder (to taste), 4 teaspoons salt, 2 teaspoons granulated sugar, and ½ teaspoon ginger. In a large kettle, sauté until tender 1 cup minced onions and 1 cup diced, pared green apples in ¾ cup

❧ 179 ❦

butter or margarine. Blend in flour mixture. Slowly stir in 1 quart chicken broth and 2 cups milk, stirring often until thick. Remove from heat.

In large skillet melt 2 tablespoons butter and add 2 pounds clean, shelled shrimp. Sauté over high flame, stirring with fork for 5 minutes. Drain and add to curry sauce. Place 1½ pounds washed mushrooms (stems removed) in shallow pan. Brush with 2 tablespoons melted butter and sauté 3 minutes. Turn, brush with 2 tablespoons butter, and sauté 3 minutes longer. Add 2 tablespoons lemon juice to curry sauce. Refrigerate. When ready to serve, reheat and serve with rice garnished with parsley. Makes 8 servings.

❧

Mrs. Thomas Callahan
MIAMI

Soufflé Baked Potatoes

Mary Jane, Miami and New York hostess, delights her husband and friends with these "lighter than air" potatoes.

Scoop out 2 cooked baked potatoes and mash with salt, pepper, cream, and 1 egg yolk. Beat white of 1 egg until stiff, and fold into potato. Refill potato shells. Add grated cheese on top and bake in moderate oven for 25 minutes.

❧

Mr. Charles T. Carey
NEW YORK

Prosciutto Ham and Figs

Sometimes elegant food can be very simple. For entertaining, Mr. Charles T. Carey, Vice President and Managing Director of the St. Regis-Sheraton Hotel in New York City, has at his disposal a gigantic kitchen under the capable direction of a bevy of outstanding chefs. Although he doesn't have to prepare dishes himself, one of his favorite appetizers at his own dinner parties for

VIPs is one of the easiest for you to prepare (marvelous when you have to pay attention to a complicated entree).

Wrap luscious fresh, ripe figs tenderly with paper-thin slices of prosciutto ham . . . and serve.

～§§～

SAMMY CAHN

BEVERLY HILLS

Hawaiian Chicken Bar B-Q

Sammy Cahn, the Academy Award-winning lyricist, calls himself "Sami Kahni" when he makes Hawaiian Chicken Bar B-Q, and declares that he uses "an ancient Jewaiian recipe." He has written this himself. He has won so many Oscars for the words he has written, we wouldn't change one.
(Use Blender)

Fill blender one-third full of peanut oil
Add one-half cup dark brown sugar
Add four or five cloves of garlic
Add fresh ground black pepper (to taste)
Add one-fourth cup of soy sauce
Add one-fourth cup of white vinegar
Add pure honey to sweeten (to taste)

(Keep repeating the above mixture until you have enough sauce to immerse the amount of chicken you wish marinated. The chicken should be quartered and marinated for at least 6 hours or more— the longer the marination the better the result. The chicken should also be turned often to ensure complete marination. It should be kept in a cool place while marinating.)

To ensure perfect results it is important that the fire be a slow fire. Because of the ingredients, the chicken will tend to seem to blacken and burn, and this can be controlled so it is a golden color if the fire is not too hot and burns low and slow. It takes between three quarters of an hour to an hour for the chicken to cook through if the fire is right. Therefore allow enough time for the fire to burn down before placing first batch (bone side down) on the fire. If you faithfully follow the above you and your guests should sit down to a meal that is sheer ambrosia.

The final touch and the bit that is showmanly and magic is the spray of a fine white sweet sauterne wine, which is applied just as the chicken is served. It is best applied with the use of a Windex spray bottle and just enough to cover the chicken with a fine mist. To conclude, watch the fire and follow the above and enjoy.

⤚§⥿⤙

MRS. JACQUES COINTREAU
NEW YORK

Ice Cream au Cointreau

Dodie, wife of the famed liqueur executive, concocted this delicious dessert.

Place a scoop of vanilla ice cream in a dish and sprinkle with 1 teaspoon dry instant Italian coffee. Pour a jigger of Cointreau over ice cream. (Chocolate ice cream may be substituted.)

⤚§⥿⤙

DICK CONLON
NEW YORK

Curried Chili

Manager of the well-known New York steak house "Gallagher's," Dick serves this chili at home.

Sauté 1 pound ground round steak in thinly sliced onions and olive oil. Add 1 can cooked kidney beans, 3 uncooked small whole tomatoes, curry powder to taste, and pinches of thyme, bay leaf, and marjoram. Add 1 can undiluted consommé or bouillon cubes and simmer on stove. If contents reduce, add more consommé.

⤚§ 182 §⥿

‹❦›

DIANA DE CORDOBA
NEW YORK

Pommes de Diana

Roumanian born Diana, a well-known hostess noted for her food, frequently serves this native Roumanian dish at her apartment in New York and her home in Mexico.

Buy 1 package strudel leaves. Place leaves on damp cloth according to directions on package, laying 2 or 3 leaves on top of each other. Cook and peel 2 large potatoes and mash with 2 large packages Philadelphia cream cheese, 2 beaten eggs, and 1½ pounds Parmesan grated cheese. Brush strudel leaves heavily with melted butter. Put mixture inside and roll. (At this point they may be put in deep freeze, wrapped in aluminum foil.) When ready to serve, put leaves on aluminum foil in moderate oven and cook until golden brown (about 10 to 15 minutes). Rolls may be cut into smaller sections if desired.

‹❦›

MRS. RAYMOND COSGROVE
PALM BEACH

Crabmeat Puree

Helen, wife of retired Avco executive, delights her many Palm Beach and out-of-town friends with this tasty and nourishing puree.

Heat together equal parts cream of tomato soup, cream of pea soup, and consommé. Add sherry, salt, and pepper to taste. Add crabmeat to soup long enough for it to warm through. (Shrimps or lobster may be substituted.)

‹❦› 183 ‹❦›

MRS. MURRAY CRAIN
CHICAGO

Pears au Caramel

A Chicago hostess, Elsa is the widow of an "Advertising Age" biggie.

Peel pears, being sure they are not too ripe or they will break up in cooking. Remove core and seeds and cut into quarters. Place in shallow baking dish close together and sprinkle generously with a layer of sugar and dot about a ½ teaspoon butter over each. Place in preheated 500° oven and bake until sugar is browned (carmelized), basting once or twice with juices. When sugar has carmelized, pour in heavy cream and blend with sugar and juices. Serve hot.

DOLORES DEL RIO
MEXICO

Gardenia Soufflé

Legend has it that former motion picture star Dolores Del Rio eats gardenias. She emphatically denies this, but has given us this rice soufflé-like dish that has all the white, creamy look of one.

In a very hot pan, put a little butter. When it is melted, add ½ pound chopped hamburger, 1 tablespoon chopped tomato, ½ tablespoon chopped onion, 1 tablespoon small seedless grapes, and 1 tablespoon chopped piñon nuts. Salt and pepper to taste and fry all together.

Soak 1 cup white rice at least ½ hour. Throw that water away and boil rice in fresh water according to directions on box. Beat 6 egg whites until stiff. Fold rice into the beaten eggs.

In a deep, well-buttered casserole, place ½ the amount of rice. Lay hamburger mixture on top and cover with the rest of the rice. Set casserole in pan of boiling water (water should come about ⅓ up side of dish). Place in preheated 350° oven for about 20 minutes. Serve with a little sugar sprinkled on top.

❧❦❧

Mrs. Carelton Dodge
Palm Beach

Russian Easter Eggs

Florence, delightful Palm Beach hostess and leader of many charity events, is the wife of a retired machinery executive. She picked up this unusual recipe on one of their world tours.

Remove pointed ends of 4 hard-boiled eggs. Scoop out yolk very carefully so that white does not break. Refill with caviar and a little minced onion. Replace end. Be sure that eggs are absolutely dry on the outside, then roll in 2 stiffly beaten egg whites and drop in hot fat. Serve hot. Other fillings may be substituted.

❧❦❧

Mrs. Edward Dorr
Chicago

Tasty Chicken Wings

Pat, widow of the late noted Chicago doctor, wouldn't be without these when her children bring their many friends home.

French fry dozens of small chicken wings. Put them in a large bowl and serve with cocktail sauce on the side.

❧❦❧

Mrs. Harry Drake
Chicago

French Fried Strawberry Fritters

Alice, socialite hostess and widow of one of Chicago's biggest real estate operators and financiers, serves these at dinner parties.

Wash, hull, and chill fresh strawberries. (Orange or pineapple sections will do as well, provided they are drained.) Prepare a pancake mix according to directions but make batter extra thick. Roll fruit in batter and take out with spoon, scooping some batter with the fruit. (If batter begins to thin, add more.) Drop in deep, hot fat and fry until golden brown.

❧❦

MRS. RUSSELL EDWARDS
NEW YORK

Rosemary—That's for Remembrance

Willette Edwards, wife of the Society Editor of *The New York Times*, writes to remind me to remind all of you to use my name-sake herb:

"Rosemary adds a marvelous flavor touch to string beans when added to the water in which they are cooked. Or mix it with garlic powder and sprinkle over a leg of lamb while it's roasting. Try it on pork chops, too, for a change."

❧❦

SADIE FEIKA
CHICAGO

Prunes au Foie Gras in Wine

During one of her 30 trips around the world seeking beautiful and rare items, Sadie Feika of the well-known Feika Imports Co. also picked up this beautiful and rare recipe while in the south of France.

Pour boiling dry white wine over dried prunes. Cover and let marinate in refrigerator for 24 hours. Remove pit and stuff with pâté de foie gras or liver paste that has been blended with a small amount of cream. Add chopped pistachio nuts. May be served hot as an accompaniment to a roast or cold as an appetizer.

❧

PEPPY FIELDS
MIAMI BEACH

Pineapple Surprise

Peppy, the well-known Miami Beach *Sun* columnist and hostess of the Celebrity Show, tells us to soften a container of pineapple sherbet until soft enough to combine with ½ can of crushed pineapple (minus liquid), orange sections and 1 tablespoon of rum. Refreeze.

❧

ROSEMARY FINE
NEW YORK

"Posie's" Yorkshire Pudding with Sausages

"Posie," in charge of public relations for United Airlines at Kennedy International Airport, is wildly enthusiastic for this dish as an after-theater supper.

Arrange 1 pound link sausages in large oven-proof skillet in wheel fashion. Beat well 2 whole eggs. Add 1 cup milk, 1 cup presifted flour, and 1 teaspoon salt and beat all together. Pour over sausages and place in preheated 475° oven for 10 minutes. Then turn oven down to 350° and bake for 25 minutes longer.

❧

MRS. JAMES FITZGERALD
CHICAGO

Hot Roquefort Bites

Dorothy, widow of Chicago's late famous and loved doctor, prepared these cocktail tidbits among dozens of others that she served at her husband's cocktail parties for his colleagues.

Mash Roquefort cheese with a little softened butter. Add a little sherry wine and a dash of Worcestershire sauce. Spread on thin crackers or toast rounds and place under broiler until hot.

❧❦❧

J. EDWARD FLEISHELL
SAN FRANCISCO

Old-Fashioned Bread Pudding

Although an attorney by vocation, Mr. Fleishell and several other noted businessmen own the fashionable Le Club restaurant. This pudding was an old family recipe that Mr. Fleishell personally taught the chef to make for the enjoyment of the patrons.

Take 2 cups of milk, ½ cup of sugar, 4 whole eggs, ⅛ teaspoon grated nutmeg, ½ teaspoon cinnamon, and a pinch of salt and put them in a blender. Then chop 2 slices of bread into ½-inch squares and add the bread to mixture. Pour into a buttered 4″ × 10″, 3-inch deep Pyrex dish. Let this remain until the bread is completely immersed and not particularly floating on top of the mixture. Sprinkle an extra bit of cinnamon on top and place in a 350° oven for 1 hour. This will make a moist bread pudding. If you desire it drier, merely add an extra slice of chopped bread. Half a cup of raisins or nuts may be added if desired.

❧❦❧

KAY GABLE
ENCINO, CALIFORNIA

Eggs in the Basket

While this was one of Kay's favorite dishes, Clark wasn't fond of eggs and so she had to add a wild dove to his plate to get him to eat this.

Toast slices of white bread very lightly and put aside. Fry 2 slices of bacon (per piece of toast) until crisp. Chop bacon and some parsley. Grate Cheddar cheese and mince onions (onions may be omitted if desired).

Separate eggs (1 per slice of bread). Beat egg whites until stiff. Preheat oven to 325°. Butter toast lightly. Spread cheese and onion on top and cover completely with egg whites. With a tablespoon, make a little nest of the whites and place yolk carefully in the center. Sprinkle bacon and parsley on top. Bake 10 minutes.

꧁꧂

Mrs. Sydney Gardner
New York

Curried Chicken Noodle Soup

Gladys, the well-known socialite and hostess, has frequent requests for this delicious soup.

Boil 2 packages Lipton chicken noodle soup mix in 6 cups of water with 2 teaspoons curry powder for 15 to 20 minutes. Let completely cool before adding 1 cup milk and the juice of 1 lemon. Put in mixer and blend until smooth. Place in refrigerator overnight. Serve cold with chopped parsley on top. Makes 6 to 8 cups.

꧁꧂

Hacienda Restaurant
New Hope, Bucks County, Pennsylvania

Cheese Hacienda

The special charm of this cheese dish for cocktails is the novel way it is served to make it look as though it were an ice cream sundae.

Using an ice cream scoop, place 3 scoops of various colored cheeses side by side in a dish and top with chopped nuts. The night I was there, they used a cream cheese flavored with horseradish for the white, a cheddar flavored with Port wine for a yellow color, and a Port du Salut colored red with beet juice for the red.

MRS. LOUIS A. HEBERT
CHICAGO

Sunday Morning Potatoes

Mary Rita, wife of the Englander Mattress executive, says this is a favorite Sunday morning brunch for her husband and daughters.

Scoop the insides from baked potatoes and fill shells with scrambled eggs and creamed mushrooms. Mash the potatoes and flute them around the top. Place in the oven long enough to warm through and brown the top.

MRS. DAVID W. HILL, JR.
ST. LOUIS, MISSOURI

Knockout Soup

Mrs. Hill is a well-known worker in charities and a girlhood friend.

> *1 can (10½ ounces) cream of mushroom soup, undiluted*
> *1 can (10½ ounces) cream of tomato soup, undiluted*
> *1½ cups milk*
> *1 can (7 ounces) red sockeye salmon, drained and flaked*
> *1 can (7 ounces) crabmeat, cleaned and flaked*
> *1 cup cream*
> *2 or 3 tablespoons dry sherry*

Combine soups with milk and heat. Add salmon and crabmeat. When heated through, add cream. Heat, but *do not boil!* Add sherry and again, heat, but *do not let boil!*

This with a salad and French bread serves four amply.

Mrs. Sidney Hill
Los Angeles

Cheese Bits

Florence, wife of a captain of Western Airlines, keeps these on hand when her husband returns from a flight (providing her son, Paul, hasn't eaten them first!).

Blend 2 cups grated sharp Cheddar cheese with ¼ pound butter, 1 cup flour, ½ teaspoon salt, and ½ teaspoon paprika. Mix thoroughly. Chill slightly. Mold 1 teaspoon of the mixture around dry stuffed olives. Bake in 400° oven about 15 minutes. Makes about 48. May be kept in deep freeze before being cooked.

Mrs. Robert Hotchkiss
Pelham, New York

Parmesan Fingers

Olivia—Libby to her friends—wife of the famed doctor of urology, brings us this easy and delightful "bit of toast."

Slice bread in finger lengths and soak in cream. Coat with grated cheese and fry quickly in deep fat or brown in oven.

Joni James
Beverly Hills

Stratacelli Soup

This well-known popular recording star and entertainer tells us to reinforce 8 cups of chicken stock with 4 cubes of chicken bouillon. Cook slightly ½ package frozen spinach, drain, and then combine with broth. Just before serving, beat 4 eggs with salt and pepper. Drip eggs through small sieve into boiling soup. Serve with Parmesan cheese on top.

Maxine Mesinger, the well-known Houston columnist, was so excited about this book that she procured this recipe for us by phoning Beverly Hills and keeping the line open while she prepared it herself to be sure she was getting it correctly.

ᴇᵍᵉ

Mrs. F. Raymond Johnson
NEW YORK

Le Pain des Pauvres (The Bread of the Poor)

The beautifully dressed Laura Johnson says this dish is called Le Pain des Pauvres because with a small quantity of meat, plus lots of ingredients, one can serve many people inexpensively.

1 pound ground beef
½ pound ground lean pork
2 slices of fresh white bread dipped for a few minutes into warm milk until it can be blended
1 big Bermuda onion finely chopped and browned in oil on slow fire
¾ cup finely chopped parsley

¾ cup finely chopped dill
1 clove garlic finely chopped (if desired—optional)
½ pound ground veal
1 can tomato sauce
½ to ¾ cup chopped almonds or Macadamia nuts
1 grated raw potato
1 cup of fresh sour cream

Put all ingredients into a mixing bowl, add 1½ teaspoons salt, ½ teaspoon black pepper, ½ teaspoon allspice, and ½ teaspoon sage. Using hands, blend well (but do not overwork the meat because that will produce a loaf too dense, too tightly packed).

Put half of the loaf into an oven dish generously greased with butter (or margarine) and shape it into an oval shape. Over it place 3 hard-boiled eggs and 6 slices of bananas or pineapple depending

ᴇᵍ 192 ᵍᵉ

on taste. Each egg should have in each side (front and back) 2 slices of fruit. Place the other half of loaf mixture over it and shape all into a nice oval shape. Bake in preheated 350° oven for 45 minutes. For the last 15 minutes raise the temperature of the oven to 400°. Makes 6 or 8 generous servings. Can be served with mushroom sauce or tomato sauce or plain.

⋅⋛⋚⋅

Mrs. Bernard Kreisler
NEW YORK

Tutti-Frutti Ice Cream

Madeline describes herself as an art collector and a "food maniac." She is also a delightful hostess.

Soften vanilla ice cream and combine with cut-up carmelized fruits, cut up marshmallows, slightly stale crumbled macaroons, and a dash of sherry. Place in deep freeze.

⋅⋛⋚⋅

Foxie Leshin
NEW YORK

Fruit Maria

Foxie Leshin, noted New York interior decorator, has named this delightful dessert "Maria," from the beautiful lyrics her son, Stephen Sondheim, wrote for *West Side Story*.

In a large casserole place the contents of a can of halved peaches, drained, and a can of large black pitted cherries, drained. Add a box of dried apricots and the rind of 1 orange, pared in strips. Pour over 1 cup orange juice and the juice of 1 lemon. Add ½ cup of brown sugar and mix together. Bake about 1 hour at 350°. When finished, cover with 2 jiggers of brandy. Serve with dab of sour cream on top.

ᶔᶘᶕ

Mrs. Richard Lippman
NEW YORK
German Red Cabbage with Apples

Lucille, wife of the well-known furniture importer and manufacturer, is also a collector of paintings and Picasso pottery.

Shred very finely a medium-size head of red cabbage. Place in heavy lidded pot with 4 pared and sliced apples, 3 tablespoons butter, ¼ cup vinegar, ⅓ cup brown sugar, 1 teaspoon salt, light pinch cayenne, and 1 cup red wine. Simmer for 2 hours in own juices on low flame.

ᶔᶘᶕ

Mrs. Patrick M. McGrady, Jr.
NEW YORK

Rejuvenated Pickles

Australian born Colleen, wife of the author of *The Youth Doctors*, invented these pickles to tease her husband.

Cut off both ends of a large pickle. Scoop out inside with a corer. Fill with salmon mousse and place in refrigerator to chill. When ready to serve, cut across in ½-inch slices. Other fillings may be used as well.

ᶔᶘᶕ

Mrs. Peter Massanisco
JACKSONVILLE, FLORIDA

Mediterranean Tomatoes

"Patty," former New York model and now the wife of a business executive, is one of Jacksonville's most beautiful and charming hostesses.

Scoop out insides of large beefsteak tomatoes and stuff with small slices of zucchini, eggplant, and chopped parsley. Sauté bread crumbs in garlic-flavored olive oil. Spoon through mixture. Place stuffed tomatoes in covered skillet without water as vegetables will make their own. Let simmer until vegetables are cooked. May be served hot or cold.

∙⸲§⸲∙

MAXINE MESINGER
HOUSTON

Shrimps in Grapefruit

This popular Houston columnist tells us to halve a grapefruit and loosen sections. Place 5 or 6 cooked and cleaned shrimp on toothpicks between sections and serve with cocktail sauce.

∙⸲§⸲∙

MRS. KAY SULLIVAN MOSKOWITZ
NEW YORK

Chicken Liver Delight

Kay, wife of the late Joe Moskowitz, 20th Century-Fox biggie, frequently serves these appetizers to her many friends in the movie industry.

Wrap a slice of bacon around a chicken liver and a slice of water chestnut. Hold with a toothpick. Place under preheated very hot broiler flame and cook until bacon is crisp.

∙⸲§⸲∙

MRS. LOUIS NIZER
NEW YORK

Chicken Divan

Mildred, wife of the nationally famous attorney and author, is herself famous as a delightful and gracious hostess.

Have ready slices of white meat of cooked chicken or turkey

and a bunch of cooked broccoli. Make a sauce of 4 tablespoons butter blended with 4 tablespoons flour. Gradually add 2 cups strong chicken stock (or chicken bouillon cubes). Cook slowly over low flame, stirring constantly until sauce thickens. When thickened, fold in ½ cup whipped cream and 2 tablespoons sherry. Season to taste with salt, pepper, and a dash of cayenne. Arrange broccoli in casserole dish and pour over ½ of the sauce. Put slices of chicken over this. To remaining sauce add ¼ cup crumbled Roquefort cheese and pour this over chicken. Sprinkle top with Roquefort cheese and place under broiler until dish is warmed through and sauce is bubbling.

❧§❧

MRS. THOMAS PARKER
WESTON, CONNECTICUT

Stuffed Frankfurters

Fontaine, former *Glamour* model and now wife of a business consultant, loves to cook these over a charcoal grill on her patio, although they are equally delicious prepared under a broiler.

Slice frankfurters half way through. Fill with pieces of sharp cheese and mustard piccalilli and wrap securely in strips of bacon. Cook until bacon is crisp.

❧§❧

MRS. NEVILLE PILLING
BRADENTON, FLORIDA

Stuffed Mushrooms

Cathie, wife of the former top executive of the Zurich Insurance Co., is now living in Florida with her retired husband, who is equally as good a cook as she is.

Buy the biggest mushrooms you can find. Wipe off with a damp cloth and remove stems. Chop stems very fine and sauté a few minutes in butter, finely chopped onions, a little chopped parsley, and minced white meat of chicken. Add bread crumbs to mixture, and when crumbs begin to brown, moisten with a little cream. Fill mushroom caps with mixture and top with bread crumbs and grated cheese. Dot with butter. Place mushrooms in lightly greased pan with a little chicken stock just covering bottoms to keep mushrooms tender. Place under low flame in broiler for 20 to 30 minutes.

❦

MRS. MYRON POLONER
NEW YORK

Bonnie's Cheese Soufflé Sandwich

"Bonnie," young New York hostess and mother, frequently serves this sandwich to other mothers while the children are playing.

Toast bread on one side and butter other side. Grate ½ pound sharp American or Cheddar cheese and add ½ teaspoon baking powder and two beaten egg yolks. Fold in 2 stiffly beaten egg whites. Put under broiler until puffed and brown.

❦

MRS. THEODORE POST
NEW YORK

Borsch à la Russe

Nadja, Russian-born New York hostess, was kind enough to give us this unusually tasty soup.

Bring 1 quart bottled borsch to a boil. Remove from fire, strain, and let cool. Beat 1 whole egg with 2 tablespoons sour cream, the juice of ½ lemon, a pinch of sugar, and salt and pepper to taste. Mix with cooled borsch and refrigerate. Just before serving, mix in 1 chopped hard-boiled egg and dried dill to taste. A small bit of sour cream may be added on top if desired.

MRS. FRANK RIGHEIMER
CHICAGO
Karen's Bridge Sandwiches

Karen, wife of one of Chicago's leading attorneys, is a devotee of bridge. Her foursome always requests these sandwiches, which are not only delicious but can be eaten during the play.

Season mayonnaise to taste with dry powdered mustard, salt, pepper, and the chopped ends of green onions. Mix with chopped hard-boiled egg and make into sandwiches.

MRS. MELVIN ROBBINS
NEW YORK
Gnocchis à la Parisienne

Mona, wife of the well-known New York attorney, brings us this dish from her native Paris.

Prepare a cream puff dough by heating 2 cups boiling water with ¼ pound butter. When boiling, add 2 cups of flour all at once. Let dough dry through over a very low flame, stirring constantly (dough must be dry enough to form a ball and not stick to pan). Then add 3 whole eggs, one by one, and mix through. Let rest for 2 hours. Make balls about the size of walnuts from the dough. Poach balls in boiling water for 10 minutes. Strain well when removing. Place in buttered Pyrex dish. Pour a cream sauce over balls. Dot with butter and sprinkle grated cheese on top. Bake in preheated 450° oven for 10 minutes.

MRS. EION SCOTT
WEST VIRGINIA
Corn Puffs

Grace, wife of the Scottish-born professor of agriculture at the University of West Virginia and one of the world's leading experts in plant pathology, has given us this old Scottish family recipe.

Place 1 cup white cornmeal into 3 cups boiling water in the top of a double boiler over low heat. Cook until cornmeal completely absorbs water and is fairly dry (about 10 to 15 minutes). Put cornmeal through sieve. Beat 5 egg whites until stiff. Fold whites into cornmeal. Drop on greased baking tin by the teaspoonful and bake in 350° oven 30 to 45 minutes or until crisp and dried out on inside. Try one before taking out of oven. Serve hot with butter or with butter and honey. Will make 40 or 50.

✎❅❧

ROGER SMITH
LOS ANGELES

Ann-Margret's Flaming Mount Fujiyama

As a bachelor, Roger cooked out of necessity, and during the three years he courted Ann-Margret, he beguiled her with his culinary efforts. Today, despite the fact that they have a cook, Roger still cooks—because he enjoys it. This is one of the delicious recipes that won Ann-Margret's heart.

Let a pint of vanilla ice cream become soft enough to mold it into the shape of a mountain (inverted cone), and place this mold into a shallow bowl. Sprinkle fresh shredded cocoanut over the mold and imbed it into the soft ice cream. Place the bowl in freezer and allow enough time before serving so that mold is frozen solid. Right before serving, fill the bowl with freshly whipped cream (the cream being the clouds at the base of Mount Fuji). Heat a good brandy, pour over the mountain, flame brandy, and serve. The brandy burns the cocoanut, giving the dessert a "burnt" taste. The real surprise is when you have eaten your way down through clouds and discover the bowl of brandy below.

✦❁✦

MRS. ALFRED STEPAN, JR.
WINNETKA, ILLINOIS

Mary Lou's Chicken Livers

Mary Lou, wife of biggie chemical manufacturer and in the vanguard of all cultural activities, is also a food connoisseur.

Soak chicken livers in milk for at least ½ hour. Remove and pat dry. Dredge lightly in flour and sauté in butter, browning on all sides. Add thinly sliced pared apples and a little sherry. Let apples brown and soften. Remove and place on warm platter. May be served with a mushroom sauce if desired.

✦❁✦

MRS. ANTHONY STORY
NEW YORK

Fuji Chicken

Judy, wife of colonel "Tony" Story, famed pilot for General Douglas MacArthur, brings us this recipe, which she learned while living in Japan.

Cut up frying chicken and marinate overnight with ½ cup soy sauce, 2 cups sugar, 2 crushed garlic cloves, salt, pepper, and ½ cup Saki (white wine may be substituted, but in that case use 1 cup). A little ginger root may be added if desired. Place in large pan in 350° oven and bake for 1 hour, turning once and basting frequently with the marinade. Chicken will be deep golden brown when completed.

✦❁✦

LESLIE UGGAMS

Bean Salad

The musical comedy and TV star frequently whips up her own version of bean salad to be served with barbecue at her home in the Doheny Estates high up over most of Hollywood.

✦ 200 ✦

For 10 or 12 people, use 2 cups cooked kidney beans, 2 cups cooked chick peas, 1 cut-up green seeded pepper, 1 large Bermuda onion sliced into rings, 1 jar cut-up pimento, 1 tablespoon oregano, a little garlic, 1 cup olive oil, ½ cup wine vinegar, and ½ teaspoon sugar. Mix all this together and marinate for 24 hours. Serve cold.

❧❦❧

ELLIE WEIDERKEHR
NEW YORK-NASSAU

Heart's Delight

The beautiful Swiss-born popular hostess has delighted us with this unusual pie dessert.

Have one meringue pie shell ready (be sure meringue is not too crisp as it will have to be sliced later). Carefully pare thin strips from orange rind of 4 large oranges (only pare from surface). Put these on on a very low fire with the juice of 1 orange, the juice of 1 lemon, and 4 tablespoons sugar. Let cook for 2 hours. Meanwhile, section the oranges, removing skin and seeds, and place in covered bowl in refrigerator along with 1 jigger cognac. Leave for 2 hours. When ready to serve, fill meringue shell with vanilla ice cream, cover with sectioned oranges (drained), top with whipped cream, and spread carmelized orange peels over cream.

❧❦❧

MRS. SIDNEY WEIL
HIGHLAND PARK, ILLINOIS

Chicken in Pineapple

Helen, the wife of the head of the Weil Plumbing Co. and a popular suburban hostess, suggests this dish for luncheons or buffet suppers.

Cut 2 pineapples lengthwise and hollow out, cubing the cut-out pineapple. Set aside. Prepare a chicken salad with a dressing of ½ mayonnaise and ½ whipped cream, seasoned with salt, pepper, and garlic to taste. Add small seedless grapes and cut pineapple and refill shells. Place the four shells in the center of the table end to end so that leaves branch out on all four sides. Sprinkle with chopped mint.

❧❦❧

MRS. DORWIN WILSON
ORLANDO, FLORIDA

Chocolate Meringues

Louise, wife of Colonel Wilson, frequently served these delicious meringues to other Army wives and their families around the world.

Place vanilla bean in ½ cup of sugar and let remain overnight. Beat 1 egg white stiff. Remove bean from sugar and add the sugar and 2 tablespoons finely grated bittersweet chocolate to egg white. Beat until sugar has dissolved. Drop by spoonful well apart on greased baking sheet and bake in 300° oven for about 10 minutes. Let cool on cake rack.

❧❦❧

MRS. GEORGE WOODS
NEW YORK

Raspberries on Raspberries

Louise, wife of the former head of the World Bank, considers this her most popular dessert.

To 1 pint of raspberries, add about 1 cup sugar (to taste) and enough water to cover. Bring to a boil, reduce heat, and cook until jamlike consistency (about 10 minutes). Let berries cool. When ready to serve, place in precooked pie shell. Cover with whipped cream and lay fresh raspberries on top of cream. Again cover with whipped cream and another layer of fresh raspberries. Cover top with chopped almonds.

INDEX